THINKING PAST TERROR

ISLAMISM AND CRITICAL THEORY ON THE LEFT

SUSAN BUCK-MORSS

VERSO

London • New York

First published by Verso 2003
© Susan Buck-Morss 2003
This edition published by Verso 2006
All rights reserved

The moral rights of the author have been asserted

1 3 5 7 9 10 8 6 4 2

Verso
UK: 6 Meard Street, London W1F 0EG
USA: 180 Varick Street, New York, NY 10014–4606
www.versobooks.com

Verso is the imprint of New Left Books

ISBN-13: 978–1–84467–562–3
ISBN-10: 1–84467–562–9

British Library Cataloguing in Publication Data
A catalogue record for this book is available from the British Library

Library of Congress Cataloging-in-Publication Data
A catalog record for this book is available from the Library of Congress

Typeset in Minion by SetSystems Ltd, Saffron Walden, Essex
Printed and bound in the USA by Quebecor World, Fairfield

For Teresa Brennan
1952–2003

This book is dedicated to the memory of Teresa Brennan, who cheered its writing, but did not see its birth. Her spirit nourishes the global public sphere to which it is addressed.

CONTENTS

ACKNOWLEDGEMENTS AND CREDITS

Thanks to Verso Press, which took on this manuscript with enthusiasm, and particularly to Tim Clark for seeing the book through to completion with enormous helpfulness and skill. For layouts and image reproductions, special thanks to go Iftikhar Dadi and Joan Sage.

Images 1–6. From *Wonder Beirut*, Joana Hadjithomas and Khalil Joreige. Courtesy of the artists.

Image 7. José Clemente Orozco, "The Dead" (*Los muertos*), 1931, Museo de Arte Carrillo Gill, Mexico City/INBA 17268.

Images 8–14. inSITE2000. See the book of the project, *Fugitive Sites*, edited by Oswaldo Sanchez and Cecilia Garza.

Image 15. Iftikhar Dadi and Elizabeth Dadi, billboard installation, 2002. Courtesy of the artists.

PREFACE

When a book is written in response to an historical event, precisely the history in it quickly recedes. The September 11 attacks on New York and the Pentagon, which were the impetus for these essays, have led to a measure of global violence that could not then have been imagined. The attacks themselves are now several wars away. A preface to the paperback edition needs to ask: When history recedes, what is left standing? What is the value of the book for readers today?

The book's central proposal is that Islamism as a political discourse can be considered together with Critical Theory as critiques of modernity in its Western-developed form. It asks readers to suspend existing political identities and reconfigure the parameters of their discourse to recognize overlapping concerns. It does this performatively, analyzing the present through the work of contemporary Islamic rather than Western theorists. Its touchstones are not Agamben, Žižek, Derrida, or Habermas, but rather, Taha, Gannouchi, Shariati, and Qutb. Three years later, these names of Muslim political theorists are scarcely more familiar to Western intellectuals than before. Despite post-colonial sensibilities to the errors of orientalist discourse, despite all the sensitivity to constructions of the Other, with few exceptions (already existing and acknowledged in the book), Western critical theorists act as if all that is necessary is to draw on their own, existing models and traditions to define any new state of the world.

If religion has been allowed back on the theoretical agenda, it is St Paul who monopolizes the discussion. For a number of important Western theorists, Pauline Christianity has suddenly become fashionable. But it is an idealized and sanitized Paul, stripped of the anti-Semitism that was a consequence of Christianity's separation from its Jewish origins, with the first Jewish anti-imperialist revolt of 66–70 C.E., and forgetful of Christianity's own imperial legacy, inherited from the Emperor Constantine, that culminated with the papal-led, medieval crusades against the Muslim world. Western philosophical traditions of the European Enlightenment, American democracy, and post-Nietzschean skepticism become conservative when deployed in a global context despite their intent, if they bolster and protect the presumption that Euro-American thinking is in advance of the rest of the world, hence adequate for its present understanding. It is one thing to champion multiculturalism in the spirit of Christian love, or Enlightenment cosmopolitanism, or democratic inclusion, or post-modern anti-essentialism; it is quite another to accept, when judged in global terms, the minority position of one's own intellectual culture, the present dominance of which cannot be explained solely on the basis of its intrinsic worth. My book is not a call for Western theorists to convert or be still. Rather, it implies the need to argue for our beliefs on truly foreign, and in many ways unpalatable, discursive terrains –just as colonized people are routinely required to do *vis-à-vis* the invading culture, just as Muslim intellectuals have done since the Napoleonic invasions several centuries ago.

The sub-title of the book, *Islamism and Critical Theory on the*

Left, was meant as a challenge, and a question: to rediscover one's own commitments in a foreign political language, and to ask not only what is lost in translation but also what might be gained. How does Islam, which defines progress in terms of social cohesion rather than individual competition, and evaluates society in civil rather than personal terms, provide a corrective for the morally indifferent world of global markets, where social responsibility is an optional appendage to political life? How does the transnational strength of Islam as a highly contemporary phenomenon expose the fact that Western norms are not natural, not inevitable, but contingent and subject to change? In the reception of the book, it is not the descriptive term Left that has proved problematic. Muslim critical theorists have been grateful for the acknowledgement that the progressive policies they espouse are fully compatible with this positioning on the political spectrum, whereas the sort of Islamic politics that appeals to transnational Muslim elites is fully compatible with the self-enriching goals of economic globalization, not to speak of the right-wing agendas of extremists on issues of military violence and sexual control (which they share with right-wing supporters of George W. Bush). Being on the Left is an orientation, not a dogma. The word makes sense wherever progressive politics requires independent judgment (*itjihad*) rather than unquestioned obedience in thought and deed. Muslim feminists are a critical part of this Left, refusing on theological, social and legal grounds to equate Islam with the patriarchal society in which it has too long been embedded. Far more controversial has been my use of the word Islamism. It was at a meeting of *l'Académie de la Latinité* in Alexandria that Dr Ahmad Jalali of Iran rightly questioned this choice, as it implies ideological conformity rather than a discursive terrain that encourages dissent and is open for creativity and change.

The fact that the first translation of this book was done in Israel (by Resling Press), followed by Greece and Japan, is rewarding. I am grateful to be included among a growing list of authors who in various ways are pushing the boundary of intellectual responsibility beyond the provincialism of the West, notably, Judith Butler, Zillah Eisenstein, Roxanne Euben, Amy Goodman, Naomi Klein, Saba Mahmoud, Arundhati Roy, and Ann Stoller. Not all of the book's essays deal directly with political Islam, but all reflect the challenge of this engagement. Acknowledging the unavoidably global resonances of any theoretical claim today, they call for an epistemological rather than ontological approach to theory, because existentially we are *not* in the same position, whereas critical judgments can be shared. Implied is a questioning of the presumption that culture is the determining factor in the construction of political subjectivities. Physical torture, bodily mutilation, civilian terror, public humiliation, arbitrary imprisonment, and the control of populations through fear – these are the physical realities of war as a human initiative, the terrors of which do not depend on cultural mediation for their meaning. The task of an artistic avant-garde in this context is defined less by achieving global recognition within the proliferating art worlds, than by positioning itself below the radar as a subaltern, globally connected underground that serves, not the warring factions, but those civilian multitudes who are caught in the crossfire. It is a mark of our time that the most radical, most difficult political position to sustain is independence from both violent sides.

A certain strand of Muslim thought has indeed become more accessible to Western readers. Liberal Islam is promoted as the responsible core of contemporary Islamic thought. Muslim reasonableness, tolerance and fairness are reassuringly presented to European and US audiences as the non-dangerous, de-politicized center. But the alternative to both terrorisms, non-state and state, is not some safe, middle position of political quietism. Progressive does not mean "like the West." In a too-eager attempt at reconciliation we lose the space for radical, critical distance from both sides in this war. For the past several years, I have taught the political theory of contemporary Islam. What happens in my seminar is not quite what the title advertises. A sustained engagement with Islamic political thinkers inevitably ends up destabilizing the students' own political identity. In discussing whether politicized Islam is compatible with democracy, their presumption of democracy in America begins to unravel. Confronting the prejudice of Western discourses of orientalism is only the beginning of this process. It is by reading the debates *among* Muslims that the students' world-orientation is most unsettled. Muslim political debates today engage divergent Islamic approaches to issues of sovereignty, national identity, legal traditions, and social justice that leave the tired category of the West out of the discussion altogether. That is far harder for US university students to bear.

What three years ago seemed implausible is now commonplace: the US population has demonstrated its support in free elections for preemptive war, government misinformation, media control, dictatorial executive powers, suspension of human rights, and violation of international and domestic laws. In the US government's identification of its own national interest with maintaining global hegemony, democracy is not the uncontroversial bedrock of political life, but merely one, expendable option in the policy toolbox. We are witnessing a test case of how far American democracy will go in agreeing to its own destruction – not the first time this has happened in the history of democratic states. The situation calls for a very different theoretical discussion than the one that has dominated in Western critical circles until now. As Muslims struggle with the issue of the legitimacy of sovereign power and its relation to religion, ethnicity and the nation-state, Western publics are doing the same. Debates about *vilayat-i-faqi* (sovereignty of the jurists) parallel those over the "state of exception" in Western democracies – if not in the substance of the arguments or the specific populations targeted by state repression, then surely in the dangers of unchecked executive power over governance and justice alike. Interpretation of *shari'a*, like constitutional judicial review, negotiates change through continuity. Both are challenged by the moral claims of global majorities who, while outside of their proper jurisdiction, are no less worthy of moral recognition. Revolutionary violence may be expressed in terms of the Mahdi, or the Messiah, or Marx, but all such legitimations of force are limited by human fallibility and historical unpredictability, and all are subject to moral scrutiny by non-adherents within the newly global, public sphere.

It seems light-years since the euphoria experienced by millions who participated in the spontaneously organized, global manifestation of February 15, 2003, against Bush's planned invasion of Iraq. That was the dream-form of a global Left. Against it, the historical realities of public responses are stubbornly intrusive: the second-term election of George W. Bush; riots in the Muslim suburbs of France; the London metro bombing; anti-immigrant xenophobia in many countries, and violent demonstrations from Pakistan to Nigeria against the Danish cartoons of the Prophet. These incidents, encoded within local political rhetoric, easily reinforce existing power while diverting it to the right, and that is precisely the problem. When the standoff between competing political powers becomes increasingly hostile and yet still claims to represent the mainstream, then the *global* center appears in these partial and polarized contexts as a radical, leftist fringe.

Nonetheless, one by one, but cumulatively in massive numbers, people are refusing to accept the traditional ways of framing global politics. Ideologies come later, if at all. Discursive articulations are secondary, as people are motivated above all by material realities. Global media have been progressive in transmitting these realities. Jean Baudrillard, in criticizing the society of the spectacle, opposes to the virtual world of media "the event," implying that only the latter can motivate a progressive, political response. For Alain Badiou, prototypical of such an event were the street demonstrations of 1968. But it needs to be remembered that these were *image–events*, effective because of their entry into media-flows that, although far from unobstructed, repeatedly escape control. Surely the images of US torture at Abu Ghraib produced such an event, as have citizen demonstrations for democracy in many countries. Global publics continue to be engaged in the production, circulation, and reception of image–events as significant political actions.

Can it be that we are at last growing up to our global responsibilities? There is a developing conviction that the proper judge for the legitimacy of sovereign foreign policy cannot be sovereign power itself, but rather, an impartial jury that also hears the case of those affected by it. To speak of a global public sphere today means to acknowledge the fact that domestic and global politics bleed into each other. Governments can no longer make a convincing moral case for limiting justice or humane treatment to the minority of humanity whom they happen to recognize as their own. Democracies are obliged to act democratically on the global stage. Islamic movements cannot limit their understanding of *itjihad* in a way that criminalizes dissent or condemns non-believers. To cite Abdul-Karim Soroush, "Religion is divine, but its interpretation is thoroughly human and this-worldly." To mimic or perpetuate Western–modern political forms is indeed backward, if these forms are revolutionary violence, state terror, or constructions of sovereign power that rely on naming an enemy for their legitimation. The revolutionary goal is a new moral template for earthly rule.

New York and Ithaca
April, 2006

INTRODUCTION

This project was not planned. The critical engagement with Islamism as a political discourse, the interrogation of global cultural practice, rethinking the Left within a global public sphere – these topics were not on my agenda before September 11, 2001. I had intended during a sabbatical leave in New York City to work on historical investigations – contributions to an "archaeology of globalization" – when the attack on the World Trade towers took place. What made it impossible to continue work, unaffected by political events, was the fact that as a US citizen I was now engaged in an unlimited war that placed civilian populations at unlimited risk, in a part of the world and from a political culture about which I was as inadequately educated as the mainstream media that informed me.

In the Government Department where I teach, there is at present no professor specializing in the Middle East. In this major knowl-edge-producing institution, Islam is understood as religion, not politics, and delegated to the department of Near Eastern Studies.[1] My own field, political theory, is based on a canon of writers that as a rule does not include non-Western political philosophers.[2] I teach Kant, Hegel, Heidegger, Adorno, and Benjamin to graduate students who come from Pakistan, Turkey, Israel, Egypt, India, Indonesia, Malaysia and elsewhere. The imbalances in this situation suddenly seemed intolerable.

Much of my year on leave from teaching was spent reading about the various political discourses that are expressed in the shared language of Islam, and that I am describing here as the discursive field of "Islamism."[3] Although scholars and practitioners vary greatly in their interpretations and evaluations, they concur in seeing this political discourse as a compelling, if troubling, critique of the way "modernity" has been experienced by millions of Mus-lims in the so-called Third World. Perhaps more than any other factor, this commonality of experience justifies describing the wide variety of contemporary Islamic politics as one discursive field. Islamism is not terrorism. It is the politicization of Islam in a postcolonial context, a contemporary discourse of opposition and debate, dealing with issues of social justice, legitimate power, and ethical life in a way that challenges the hegemony of Western political and cultural norms.

Like nationalism, liberalism, feminism, and socialism, Islamism frames social and political debates without preempting their content. Islamist extremists are militantly violent.[4] But Islamism in its origins is first and foremost a critical discourse articulated by intellectuals and educators, often at great personal risk, and their analytical insights merit discussion and debate within a global public sphere by non-Muslims and Muslims alike.[5] Social movements that express themselves within Islamist discourse are frequently in opposition to each other, as their forms of activism span the entirety of the known political spectrum – from terrorist networks, to right-wing authoritarianism, to neo-liberal centrism, to left-radicalism, to secular-state egalitarianism, to guerrilla warfare. The political impact of Islamism, far from monolithic, has been reactionary, conservative, democratic, revolutionary, conspiratorial – depending on the specific and changing national and international contexts in which Islamism has developed over a period of several generations.

One might have hoped that in the "democratic" United States the media would have educated audiences regarding Islamist discourses in all of their political variations and historical complexities. But in the heavy atmosphere of patriotism and military preparedness that was generated after the September 11 attacks, in-depth understanding was not on the national agenda. It would have entailed revisiting in more than a cursory manner the multiple cases of CIA support for violently extremist Islamist groups, as well as for paramilitary government violence in the Middle East – historical facts of US Cold-War policy that do not fit into the Bush administration's simplified scenario of good versus evil.

In Europe and elsewhere, the public has been better served. But even in the United States, alternative voices have not been silent. Noam Chomsky's book, 9–11, which details the historical background and global context of the event, sold extensively to a media-saturated but information-starved public.[6] The internet has demonstrated its significant and salutary power to correct the distorted picture of mainstream media, making possible the circulation of work by Chomsky, Edward Said, Avraham Oz, Arundhati Roy, and many others, as well as information posted by newly established collectives throughout the world. Without such critical media, no sane, global discussion would be possible.

This book presumes the existence of global information networks, and asks how political imagination might be effectively transformed because of them. It takes on the challenge of thinking past terror in order to engage a global public that rejects both forms of violence, terrorist and counter-terrorist alike. Those of us who count ourselves a part of this public – we are quite plausibly the majority – fit poorly into the definitions that have been offered. Against social science that allots to us the partial and self-interested role of individual "rational actors," we understand ourselves as social beings for whom reason is a normative, moral term. Against identity theories that preach the incommensurability of global publics, such moral reason is necessarily autonomous from any partial collective that holds itself superior and impervious to critique. In a global public sphere, tolerance is the first criterion: we cannot be placed on the defensive because of who we are. Freedom of dissent is the second: we need to be able to criticize power that is inhuman in its effects, regardless of the identities of those who exercise it. The third criterion defines the goal: to trust each other politically and to act together, even when the languages in which we speak our moral concerns not only differ, but seem to be in open contradiction.

What this means – and we are all still far too provincial to cope with the implications – is that democracy on a global scale necessitates producing solidarity beyond and across the discursive terrains that determine our present collective identifications. The goal is not to "understand" some "other" discourse, emanating from a "civilization" that is intrinsically different from "our own." Nor is it merely organizational, to form pragmatic, interest-driven alliances among pre-defined and self-contained groups. Much less is it to accuse a part of the polity of being backward in its political beliefs, or worse, the very embodiment of evil. Rather, what is needed is to rethink the entire project of politics within the changed conditions of a global public sphere – and to do this democratically, as people who speak different political languages, but whose goals are nonetheless the same: global peace, economic justice, legal equality, democratic participation, individual freedom, mutual respect.

As political events unfold, the foggy term "globalization" becomes clearer. Whereas modernization as a narrative placed national units on a temporal continuum from "backward" to "advanced," globalization does not presume the historical time of Western progress. Global space entails simultaneity, overlap, coherencies incoherently superimposed. Like a photograph in multiple exposure, it makes sense only precariously, only by blocking out part of the visible field. We are capable of seeing further than is comprehended by our separate, sense-making practices, and what we see limits the legitimacy of what we do.

Some examples: As a rational Cold-War strategy, it makes sense that the US supported bin Laden's Afghan-based warriors as "freedom fighters" against the Soviet Union, exposing them to the methods of counterinsurgency – arms deals, assassinations, drug trade-routes, laundered money, false identities, secret conspiracies – that they now use against their former benefactors. Within the imaginary terrain of global capitalism, the benefits of free trade and economic interdependence seem self-evident, but only if the environmental and social disasters that are its consequence remain out of the conceptual frame. In Muslim countries, Islamists struggle for autonomy from "Westoxification," while their economic base fuels a global economy that is toxic to us all. Western academics and policy-makers study the "exceptionalism" of the Middle East to explain why democracy fails to develop, without asking how their treatment of these nations and their citizens as less than equal players is a failure of democracy at another level.

While each stratum of the global public sphere struggles for coherence, the whole is marked by contradictions. We coexist immanently, within the same discursive space but without mutual comprehension, lacking the shared cultural apparatus necessary to sustain sociability. We are in the same boat pulling against each other and causing enormous harm to the material shell that sustains us. But there is no Archimedean point in space at which we could station ourselves while putting the globe in dry-dock for repairs – no option, then, except the slow and painful task of a radically open communication that does not presume that we already know where we stand.

This is not to say that translation among political languages is easily accomplished. Real differences exist. But promise lies in the apparent incommensurabilities, because the attempt forces each language to extend itself creatively, becoming more than it was, producing an open space in which a new politics might take root. I have in mind the work of Talal Asad. His analysis of the Salman Rushdie Affair was unexpected.[7] As an anthropologist and a Muslim, born in the Middle East and teaching in the United States, he turned his academic attention not to the culture of the Islamic clerics who condemned this writer for blasphemy, but to the condemnation by Britain's liberal elites of its own Muslim citizenry, thereby exposing the degree to which British tolerance continues to presume the outsider status of those tolerated. He did this in no way to sanction the "shocking" *fatwa* that jeopardized Rushdie's life.[8] Rather, his implication was that cultural confrontations are not to be resolved by the triumph of a more civilized "West" over others, but by the recognition of partialities in all of our behaviors – a very different lesson, and a civilizing one. What enlightened me in reading Asad's book was coming upon the name of the intellectual who has most influenced my work, the critical theorist Walter Benjamin, whom he cites as theoretical support for his endeavor.

A successful translation, Benjamin wrote in the 1920s when he was translating Baudelaire's poetry into German, leaves neither the original nor the receiving language unchanged. Asad comments on Benjamin's text with cultural translation in mind: "The relevant question therefore is not how tolerant an attitude the translator ought to display toward the original author (an abstract ethical dilemma) but how she can test the tolerance of her own language for assuming unaccustomed forms."[9] If we understand the task of translation as a political project, then the treatment of political languages as *mutually* open to transformation challenges the unequal arrangements of global power.[10] It is by definition a project on the Left.

In the 1970s when I was a student, Marxism in its multiple variants – Western Marxism, Marxist humanism, Trotskyism, Leninism, Maoism, Fanonism – provided the common discursive terrain in which critics of exploitation and domination could agree (often vehemently, even violently) to disagree. The secular Left throughout the Middle East was a vibrant part of that conversation. A comparison informs us as to how the discourse of the new global Left will be different from the Marxist international one, where translation occurred, but heavily in one direction. Any Leftist who lived in or visited the "undeveloped" world at that time will be aware of the degree to which the Marxist Left understood itself as an avant-garde in elite terms, rather than popular and democratic. Despite their radically critical stance, Marxists embraced a vision of modernization that had in common with capitalism and imperialism a conception of the Third World as inexorably backward and behind.[11] Part of postcolonial reality since the end of the Cold War has been the disintegration of the discursive unity provided by Marxism, for which some of us must confess feeling not a small bit of nostalgia. What is gained, however, is more valuable. If the language of the global Left is not presumed, but struggled for in open communication, if the Leftist project is itself this struggle, then democracy defines its very core.

Critical theory and Islamism offer one nodal point for such a translation, which is a project of central concern to several of the essays in this book (Chapters 2 and 5). Addressing the critical discourses of Islamism that are unknown within the school of critical theory in which I was trained has meant confronting my own infinite ignorance when judged in a global context. I am grateful to Asad, who gave back to me Walter Benjamin, enriched by the use he made of his work, and to the great number of Muslim intellectuals writing in the United States and Europe who have been involved in the project of cultural translation for decades. Their writing made entry into the discussion possible.

■

As a critical theorist, I travel in one coherent stratum of global space, centered in and dominated by the West but with outposts elsewhere – we can call it the "theoryworld." It closely resembles the now very prominent "artworld," with which it sometimes overlaps. I have been involved in the artworld for several years, recently as curator of inSITE2000, a site-situated art project in Tijuana and San Diego at the Mexican/United States border. The challenge in writing theory for the artworld is somehow to avoid the inevitable promotional role – theory endorsing art; art illustrating theory – producing a circular coherence that insulates itself from criticism even as it enacts critique. (Artworld and theoryworld, alternative terms for cartels of symbolic capital, are examples of the cultural inequities of globalization.) It was by engaging Islamism and struggling with political translation that I was able to find a voice outside of this circularity, one that has nothing to do with Islam, but everything to do with the possibility of a critical, global public sphere and cultural practices within it (Chapters 3 and 4). Two processes of cultural politics – escaping the gated communities of the artworld and theoryworld to address the larger public sphere, and struggling to engage a theoretical discourse, Islamism, not democratically represented within it – turned out to be part of the same intellectual endeavor.

Through working with inSITE2000 I came to know Catherine David, the creative and socially committed curator, presently Director of Witte de With in Rotterdam, who well before September 11 had initiated an ongoing project of seminars and exhibitions called "Contemporary Arab Representations."[12] She placed me in contact with artists whose work it seemed relevant to include in this text. Several of the images reproduced here, including the remarkable cover, are from "Wonder Beirut" by Joana Hadjithomas and Khalil Joreige. This project contains a series of "postcards" – photographs subjected to the distorting heat of fire – embedded in a story, "The Novel of a Pyromaniac Photographer." Images of the city as a tourist destination are transformed into records of the devastation of Beirut during a decade of civil war (the realities of which make it clear that the massive urban devastation of September 11 was far from unique). The reconstruction of Beirut is a commercial attempt to recapture the city's tourist image and secure its economic niche in the global economy, entailing the obliteration of historical evidence of the war, images of which remain burned in the memories of the inhabitants.

I have included the intriguing work of artists Iftikhar and Elizabeth Dadi, who are part of the circle brought together by Salah Hassan, Chair of the Cornell Department of the History of Art and Visual Studies. Also included are images from inSITE2000 projects by Mexican and US artists – and some "found" images as well. The images are presented in counterpoint to each other and to my text. The dialogic principle of these image-interfaces allows the superimposed truths of partial perspectives to be kept in view. Rather than forcing the homogeneity of differences under overarching rubrics of human universality or the art-idea of "the family of man," the incoherence, the ruins, the ruptures in the global terrain remain visible.

Islamism and avant-garde art: In the safe space of a book (if only there), *les extrêmes se touchent*. But I will not be surprised if the creativity of both artists *and* religious theorists flourish in an open, global public sphere, because both need freedom to work against the grain, and specifically against the preemptive exclusions of identity politics – to think, Theodor Adorno would say, the "non-identical," a process, Fazlur Rahman would say, of *ijtihād* (personal reasoning) that engages the "critical spirit" of "free intellectualism," which is "genuinely Islamic and creative."[13] In the religious no less than the secular realm, cultural creativity is not reducible to endorsing a political or marketing line. If we are to think our way to a future different from the insensate scenario of unlimited warfare that has been prescribed for us, then culture needs to imagine alternative forms that are not even dreams at present – produced for a public that extends beyond the initiates, and "political" in the sense of relevant to worldly affairs – with confidence that a truly unforced cultural project will be free of both the fundamentalist intolerance and the commercial libertinism that, from partial perspectives, are now so feared.

It will be evident that the global public sphere to which I allude is not that created by global media as they are now constituted. Nor do Islamist states currently in existence provide the freedom essential for a global Left. Lacking a homeland, such a project may first consist of a radically cosmopolitan republic of letters and images, electronically connected, digitally displayed, and also circulating as books-in-translation. The contradiction of such a project, which needs to be made productive, is that it will rely on the protection of the very enclaves of freedom – academic and cultural institutions – that at present keep intellectual work isolated from political effect.

■

If the political advantage of translation is the expansion of the discursive field, then the greatest gains will be had where the differences seem to be the most extreme, while problems may lie where the task of translation confronts too little resistance. As an example, "Islamic economics" has integrated itself quite completely into the global, capitalist economy. The Pakistani economist Muhammad Akram Khan writes that Islamic economic thinking, constrained by lack of "intellectual freedom" and a fear of "dissenting opinion," has been focused far too narrowly: "The entire enterprise of Islamic banking has become a doubtful proposition, more devoted to literalist or legalistic solutions, satisfying theologians but not yielding any benefit to humanity"; it is too exclusively concerned with "material betterment to the neglect of the environment and distribution of income and equity among the people."[14] Olivier Roy states bluntly: "[T]he 'Islamic bank' is a marketing tool and not a scheme for a new economic order. . . . The Islamization of the economy is thus largely rhetorical."[15] This is despite the fact that, as Rahman insists: "The basic élan of the Qu'ran" is its "stress on socioeconomic justice and essential human egalitarianism."[16] A thought-experiment: What if the "Islamic economy" did not take the easy way of identity politics, defining itself as an economy belonging exclusively to Muslims, but considered its natural constituency to include the anti-globalization movement as the most authentic, contemporary political expression of Islamic principles regarding nature, labor and economic justice? If we are to speak in terms of a global Left rather than regime-change within Muslim countries, what may be needed is not less religious reasoning, but more.

Nothing, we are told by Western hegemonic discourse, so differentiates "us" from "them" as the lack of freedom for women in Islamist societies.[17] It needs to be noted, however, that far from silencing the power of women, Islamist regimes highlight it, acknowledging through severe and violent restrictions that what women do is crucial to political and social order. The argument justifying the strict codes of conduct, based on respect for women (in contrast to the "Western" commodification of women and their disparagement as sex objects), has a dialectical dynamic that can lead to its own undoing.[18] In the revolutionary context of Iran, where Islamist discourse has been hegemonic for several decades, women have called, legitimately, on the principles of Islam for support in demanding legal equality, divorce reform, reproductive rights, equality in the workforce, and social recognition as political activists, members of parliament, professionals, and producers of culture and the arts. Iranian women as the avant-garde of progressive Islamism are crucially influential in the present reformist tendency toward social liberalization. In Iran, in a revolutionarily violent fashion that one may hope does not need to be repeated elsewhere, two social elements traditionally fused in Muslim societies are being pried apart: Islam and patriarchy. By making it clear that they are not identical, the success of Islamist feminists in achieving their goals is one with the liberation of Islam from entrapment in patriarchal domination.

Nowhere is the task of translation as difficult, and as crucial, as among feminists at this time. Radical, cosmopolitan feminists – indeed, women on the Left generally – are demonstrating that it is they who are most open to listening and communicating, expanding their language as they learn, without compromising their principles or abandoning their progressive critiques. I speak of the incomparable Zillah Eisenstein, who responded immediately to the September 11 attacks by engaging Islamist feminisms, struggling on the basis of their varied experiences to expand her understanding of feminism in its multiplicity *and* its singularity.[19] Creative innovation based on translation also characterizes the work of Teresa Brennan, who as a Marxist economic theorist has committed the primal act of apostasy by taking religious discourse seriously in her brilliant critique of the global ecological disaster.[20] Let me acknowledge, too, the Muslim women who have responded with warmth and candor to my own project: Saba Mahmood, Haifaa G. Khalafalla, and Hanan Ibrahim, whose work and trust have been extended to me during the writing of this book.

The essays in this volume were written for specific, largely academic occasions to which I contributed during the time I was reading about the discourses of Islamism, and they took the opportunity to consider how these occasions might themselves need to be rethought. Chapter 1, written soon after the events of September 11, spoke to the political urgency of the moment by attempting to address a not-yet-existing global public sphere, against the academic expectations of the London conference sponsored by the journal *Radical Philosophy* at which it was delivered. Chapter 2 began as a contribution to a New York University "reunion" of critical theorists who work in the tradition of the Frankfurt School, and was intended as a provocation in response to the question of the conference: "How Does Critical Theory Matter Now?". Chapter 3, delivered at the Museo Carrillo Gil in Mexico City, presses the social irrelevance of the artworld and theoryworld to the point of calling for a global counter-culture. Chapter 4, written for the inSITE2000 catalogue as a curatorial postscript, interprets artists' projects as attempts to escape from the artworld; the catalogue, or "book," is entitled *Fugitive Sites.* Chapter 5 drops the academic veil completely and speaks directly to the possibilities of a global Left. Chapter 6 is from an interview-exchange with Laura Mulvey and Marq Smith of the *Journal of Visual Culture*; it addresses the difficulties of critical theorizing as a public intellectual given the constraints of normal science in the humanities. The introduction, written just before I returned to teaching, can also be read as the book's conclusion.

■

A final, biographical moment figures in the project. By coincidence, in September 2001, I was already reading about the Middle East and recent Arab intellectual history, in anticipation of contributing to a conference at Georgetown University in honor of my dissertation advisor, Hisham Sharabi. A critical and secular scholar, Sharabi's writings analyze contemporary Arab thought and society;[21] but as professor of European intellectual history, he taught me the modern Western canon. A Left-Palestinian with a great appreciation for Western Marxism, he was the enthusiastic supervisor of my research on the German-Jewish Leftists Adorno, Benjamin and others of the Frankfurt Institute, who influenced a generation of cosmopolitan "critical theorists." (My dissertation defense took place in Lebanon just before the civil war, where Sharabi was on his sabbatical leave as visiting professor at the American University of Beirut.) The interruption in overseas transport caused by September 11, 2001, necessitated postponing his retirement conference until April. What would have been the first essay in this book, becomes the next-to-last.

It is increasingly plausible that the status quo of power has no desire to see a refiguration of the old, transnational Left as a global

Left, and that there will be, at least in the United States, an attempt to brand all progressive resistance to the "war on terror" as directly or indirectly on the side of the terrorists. Nothing could be further from the truth. Terrorism will disappear because non-violent ways of communication and debate are possible. The essays written here are meant to contribute to that goal.

This is a little book. It makes a very small contribution. But without the freedom and facilities of my profession even it would have been impossible. I hope that readers who have not had the time and resources available to me will find it useful.

Ithaca, New York
September, 2002

NOTES

1. Such categorization is typical in US universities, despite the fact that the majority of Muslims do not live in the Near East (four-fifths of Muslims are non-Arabs).
2. This situation is being challenged by the salutary call for the study of "comparative political philosophy." See Roxanne Euben, *Enemy in the Mirror: Islamic Fundamentalism and the Limits of Modern Rationalism* (Princeton: Princeton University Press, 2001).
3. The term is itself politically charged, and its use in the literature is contested. In Western discourses it may function problematically as a new form of Orientalism, defining the political beliefs of Muslims as radically "other" than Western ideals. My argument in Chapter 5 is precisely opposed to that position. Sympathetic scholars speak of an "Islamic Revival," or use the term "political" or "politicized" Islam, out of concern that "Islamism" may reify the phenomenon in a pejorative way, giving the misimpression of a monolithic and fixed ideology. Others delimit the subject matter to focus only on Islamic "fundamen-

talism," suggesting comparisons with other religious fundamentalisms worldwide. Among activists, many are comfortable defining themselves as "Islamists" (Egypt's "New Islamists," for example) while others are not, preferring terms like "progressive" or "traditional" Islam, that describe a political orientation as much as a political language. Those whom I call "Islamist" writers themselves express the view that their contemporary interpretation *is* Islam in its renewed and "authentic" form.

4. The terrorist organization of al-Qaeda is not representative of even these extremists, the majority of whom are struggling on a national level against repressive regimes for self-determination, or simply for inclusion within the political process.

5. Influential writers who demonstrate the diverse thinking within Islamist discourse and whose texts were (partially) available to me in English translation include: Mohammed Arkoun (Algeria/France), Rachid Al-Ghannouchi (Tunis/London), Imam Ruhullah al-Musavi al-Khomeini (Iran), Muhammad Iqbal (India/Pakistan), Sayyid Qutb (Egypt), Fazlur Rahman (Saudi Arabia/Pakistan/USA), Ali Shariati (Iran), and Mahmoud Mohamed Taha (Sudan). All of these writers were cosmopolitan in their personal lives, most were educated at least in part in the "West" (some lived there in exile), and several have been Western academics (Arkoun at the Sorbonne; Rahman at the University of Chicago).

Their fates indicate the extreme diversity of Islamist contexts: Both Qutb and Taha were executed for their political views, but Qutb was the victim of Nasser's secular-nationalist regime in Egypt, while Taha was tried and executed by Sudanese President Numeiri as part of the latter's policy of imposed Islamization; Shariati's death in London was quite possibly the act of the Iranian secret police under the Shah, while Khomeini, who spent part of his exile in Paris, became the religious head of the Islamic Republic of Iran. Iqbal, who studied at Cambridge and Heidelberg, was recognized after his death as the national poet and spiritual father of Pakistan. The innovatively modern interpretations of Islam by Arkoun and Rahman were nourished by the freedom and resources of Western academic institutions; Rahman was briefly active in the government of Pakistan. Arkoun, a Berber, has been consistently an independent academic, keeping his distance from both Western Orientalism and Islamist activism. Al-Ghannouchi, educated in Cairo, Damascus and France before he returned to Tunisia as a radical activist, was imprisoned twice and sentenced thrice, before exile in London, where he became the leader of the "Islamic Renaissance Movement." Al-Ghannouchi's influential writings argue on the basis of Islam for individual freedoms, free elections, and a multiple (including communist) party system.

6. Noam Chomsky, *9–11* (New York: Seven Stories Press, 2001).

7. Talal Asad, "Multiculturalism and British Identity," *Genealogies of Religion: Discipline and Reasons of Power in Christianity and Islam* (Baltimore and London: The Johns Hopkins University Press, 1993).

8. Asad, *Genealogies of Religion*, p. 239.

9. Ibid., p. 190.

10. "The inequality of languages is a feature of the global patterns of power created by modern imperialism and capitalism. . . . My argument is directed against the assumption that translation requires the adjustment of 'foreign' discourses to their new site. In my view, they should retain what may be a discomforting – even scandalous – presence within the receiving language" (ibid., p. 199).

11. See Ali Mirsepassi, *Intellectual Discourse and the Politics of Modernization: Negotiating Modernity in Iran* (New York and Cambridge: Cambridge University Press, 2000), pp. 36–53.

12. See the volume *Tamáss: Contemporary Arab Representations* (Barcelona: Fundació Antoni Tàpies, 2002), also the website: http://www.uia.es/artpen/world. "To escape from the patronizing and opportunistic attitude with which the works and ideas of contemporary creators linked to the Arab world are presented, is one of the most fundamental aims of this seminar. What interests us," underlines Catherine David, "is the emancipating potential of their proposals, their capacity to question from a radical and experimental perspective the social and cultural discourses that surround them. It is not a question of valuing things from an evolutionary western historicism which frequently leads to sterile formalism."

13. Fazlur Rahman, *Islam and Modernity: Transformation of an Intellectual*

Tradition (Chicago: The University of Chicago Press, 1982), pp. 11, 129. For Rahman, referring specifically to Islam, "the process of questioning and changing a tradition. . . . can continue indefinitely." He cites al-Shatibi (d. 1388) who described consensus as not only temporary, but "*mutually corroborative*," "adduced from places that are innumerable" and "from different kinds of sources which cannot be reduced to a single type" (al-Shatibi, cited in ibid., p. 22). The need for a creative interpretation of Islam, and hence for intellectual freedom to engage in scholarly work, is emphasized as well by Mohammed Arkoun (see *Rethinking Islam: Common Questions, Uncommon Answers*, trans. and ed. Robert D. Lee (Oxford: Westview Press, 1994). Both found that freedom in Western universities, where they taught and contributed to academic culture. My use of the term "Islamist" to include their creative scholarship stresses the fact that Islamism as a critical discourse of modernity is not coterminous with any particular political unit or part of the world.

14. Muhammad Akram Khan, "Islamic Economics: The State of the Art," *The American Journal of Islamic Social Sciences* 16, 2: 89–104.

15. Olivier Roy, *The Failure of Political Islam*, trans. Carol Volk (Cambridge, Mass. and London: Harvard University Press, 1994), p. 144.

16. Rahman, *Islam and Modernity*, p. 19.

17. On the limits and partialities of understanding in the West-liberal vision, see Charles Hirschkind and Saba Mahmood, "Feminism, the Taliban, and Politics of Counter-Insurgency," *Anthropological Quarterly* 75, 2 (Spring 2002): 339–54.

18. Foucault's insights are relevant here: No modern political phenomenon can match Islamism for "putting into discourse" the position of women. Women's dress has become a "technology of power," both as a statement of protest and a means of authoritarian control. Islamic law has generated a voluminous "regime of discourses" that Muslim women have learned to use to their advantage in judicial cases. See Michel Foucault, *The History of Sexuality*, vol. 1: *An Introduction*, trans. Robert Hurley (New York: Vintage/Random House, 1980).

19. See Zillah Eisenstein, "Feminisms in the Aftermath of September 11," *Social Text 72*, 20, 3 (Fall 2002), 79–100, and the book tentatively titled

Who is the West? Feminisms, Slaveries, Democracies, Islamisms (London: Zed, 2004).

20. Teresa Brennan, "The Critique of Judgement" (unpublished manuscript, sent to me by the author shortly before her tragic accident, a deep loss for the global Left). Of course, religion has been crucial to Western traditions of radical egalitarianism, from the movement to abolish slavery, to the US civil rights movement, to liberation theology in Latin America; Marxist atheism was often more apparent than real.

21. See especially Hisham Sharabi, *Arab Intellectuals and the West: The Formative Years, 1875–1914* (Baltimore: The Johns Hopkins University Press, 1970); *Neopatriarchy: A Theory of Distorted Change in Arab Society* (New York and Oxford: Oxford University Press, 1988); (ed.), *Theory, Politics, and the Arab World* (New York and London: Routledge, 1990).

1. "Postcard of War #2/18. Based on General Weygand Street, Beirut" from "*Wonder Beirut: The Story of a Pyromaniac Photographer*" by Joana Hadjithomas and Khalil Joreige.

ONE

A GLOBAL PUBLIC SPHERE?*

September 11 has transformed irrevocably the context in which we as intellectuals speak. The acts of terror on that day were no invasion from the outside by a barbaric evil "other" but were, rather, produced fully within a coeval and common world. We are witnessing the mutation of a new, global body-politic, and if we intellectuals are to have any potency as part of its thinking organ, it will be in discourses that refuse to separate academic life from political life, and that inform not just national opinion, but a global public debate.

To think and write for a global public sphere is not an easy task.

* This chapter was presented at the conference of the journal, *Radical Philosophy*, London, November 7, 2001, and first published in the journal, No. 111 (January/ February 2002).

I have no political choice but to try, however, as the commitment to a diverse, many-centered human society is what my work, and much critical, theoretical work, have been about for the past several decades, in universities that are now becoming decisively, and quite hopefully, global communities of scholars. The global public sphere in a broader sense, however, is not yet a "community," or even a coherently navigable discursive terrain. To address it is thus a performative act. It aims to bring about that which it presumes.

The notion of the "global" itself circulates globally today, describing and generating discourses of social change. Many, including myself, have questioned its newness, pointing to the five hundred years of European expansion that produced a world economy and world political domination. But the global terrain that is emerging out of the ruins of September 11 and its aftermath is, arguably, of a different order. And this difference has fundamentally to do with intellectual vision – what we see, and how we see it.

Historical rupture is a jagged process. There has not been a clean break with the past, there never is. The end of the Cold War, the restructuring of transnational capital, the electronic media revolution – these transition markers have been with us for decades. We have charted their development with concepts like post-modernism, post-colonialism, post-socialism, post-Marxism. But recent events bring the realization that in using these terms, our academic "global community" has not gone far enough. The hegemonic signifiers of Western capitalism, Enlightenment modernity and national sovereignty were kept in place. Radical criticism attacked their Eurocentricity without denying it. It appears now that events have outrun us, captured in a videotaped image of destructive fury that left us speechless, devastating our imagined political landscape. What disappeared on September 11 was the apparent invulnerability, not only of US territory, but of US, and, indeed, Western hegemony.

A new, global struggle for hegemony is underway. But let us not be content just to describe this process, as if the only actors who counted were military men, terrorists and counter-terrorist forces. In fact their use of force indicates their lack of hegemony, not its guarantee. It is, ultimately, the global public that will determine hegemonic power – a public newly forming, for whom the old economic and political narratives, even critical ones, are inadequate interpretive tools.

The staging of violence as a global spectacle separates September 11 from previous acts of terror. The dialectic of power, the fact that power produces its own vulnerability, was itself the message. This distinguishes it decisively from radical social movements that aim to accomplish specific social and political goals. The Chiapas resistance movement, which was violent but minimally so, used global channels in order to garner wide support from a public inside and outside of Mexico, in order to bring pressure to bear on the Mexican state to change specific policies. It was and continues to be a radical, cosmopolitan articulation that translates indigenous cultural experience into hegemonic discourses of criticism as the precondition for the intelligibility of its demands. The goal is to communicate within the existing codes of oppositional struggle. A poet, Subcomandante Marcos, speaks in its name in inclusive, human terms against diverse manifestations of oppression; solidarity for this local struggle is imagined in global terms.

In contrast, the destruction of September 11 was a mute act. The attackers perished without making demands. They left no note behind, only the moving, deadly image, which the cameras of those who were attacked themselves supplied, as they did the fuel-loaded, civilian planes that mutated suddenly into self-annihilating weapons. A mute act, played and replayed before a global audience – a message, sent by satellite to the multitude – a diversity of peoples who, witnessing the same cinematic time-image, the same move-ment-image, exploded into enemy camps.

Or did they? Sympathy was felt generally by the global public sphere. Is not the adequate word rather "implosion," as a global terrain means that there is no outside, while there is, tragically, no cohesion among the multitude who inhabit it? All the forces of global society, however radically incompatible, are immanent within this overdetermined, indivisible terrain.[1]

Communicative acts demand a code, we are told; but only one? The force of these images was that they entered simultaneously multiple fields of communication within the global public sphere, with highly varied meanings, from terror to triumph. It was not only, or even primarily, to Americans that the act was addressed. Indeed, toward Americans the aim was less to communicate than to explode understanding, a weapon of sabotage with devastating effects because, like an email virus, to receive the communication had the consequence of destroying the code. For us as Americans, to open ourselves to this message as meaningful necessitated con-scious acceptance of realities – 5 percent of the Iraqi population destroyed by US attacks and the ongoing embargo, persistent US opportunism in its Middle East foreign policy, double standards of political, economic and human rights, support for Israel despite its colonialist oppression of Palestine – realities that have been in front of our eyes and ears for decades, but that the code of American self-understanding with its master signifier of innocence had effectively blocked out as meaningless. The repeated question after September 11, "Why do they hate us?" did not want an answer. More than a rhetorical question, it was a ritual act: to insist on its unanswerability was a magical attempt to ward off this lethal attack against an American "innocence" that never did exist.

September 11 ripped a hole in the American psyche. But it was possible, even in the desolation, to see an opening to a different collective sense of self, the hope of leaving the counterfeit innocence of America behind. While New York City is on American soil, it belongs to the world, not just as a node in a network of global cities but as a place to work and live. An extreme diversity of national, ethnic, and religious communities calls it home. Imperfect, conflicted, a place of struggle, New York is a really existing, global public sphere in the most concrete and, currently, most optimistic sense. And when the rescue effort immediately began, these urban dwellers acted together without thinking separate agendas, performing heroically in the name of the diverse multitude of New Yorkers. They give me courage to write.

On September 11 the stabilizing structures of the global society that for better or worse keep the global order going proved themselves vulnerable in the highest degree. The attack exposed the fact that global capitalism is inadequately imagined as deterritorialized. Just as "the state" would reveal itself during the anthrax incident to consist of postal workers walking their delivery routes, so "capital" showed itself after September 11 as working people facing job layoffs without a union for support. The World Trade Center towers were a symbol; but they were also a human and material reality, and the photographically mediated experience of the attack was of both the symbol and the real, antagonistically superimposed.

"Photography is a theological technology," Peter Osborne tells us, because it is indexical, a trace marking the intelligibility of the material world.[2] This trace is the surplus that escapes even multiple meanings of the intentional message sent, in this case, by the terrorists. It is "theological" precisely not in the fundamentalist sense. The latter appeals to the text, whether Bible or Qur'an, to interpret the world as fateful intention. To do so is to exclude photography's material trace, the meaning of which surpasses the predetermination of the word. The traumatic intensity of the images of destruction existed precisely here: as cinematic as they appeared, they were unintentionally actual, irrefutably material and real. And the reality muddied the symbolic message.

If we are to read the act symbolically as an attack on global capital, then how do we square this with the fact that it was the secretaries, janitors, food servers, clerical workers, security guards, and firemen who were killed? If it was an attack on "America," then why were there so many other citizen nationals and so many different ethnic names among the victims? If this was the hub of the global economy, then why was it small-business people and laid-off workers who suffered? If New York was symbolic of Western cultural decadence and sexual libertinism, then why were so many ordinary friends, families and children left behind?

To see a photograph as purely symbolic, rather than as a trace of the real, is a reductive visual practice – shall we call it visual fundamentalism? Of course, this practice precisely describes the American reception of photographs of the Gulf War a decade ago: "smart" bombs that exploded human vehicles, houses and bridges like computer-game targets; retreating Iraqi troops massacred as they fled; Iraqi women sobbing in grief for family members lost in the brutal US bomb-raid on Amiriya bunker in Baghdad. On September 11, these images surged back into memory, and with them a ghost-like presence, the home-grown, Midwestern terrorist, the Gulf War veteran, the "perfect soldier" who, with reference to the US-caused death of Iraqi children, spoke with bitter irony of the Oklahoma City children he killed as "collateral damage," and who when interrogated by police answered according to US military instructions for captured prisoners of war.[3] No one in the US quite dared to mention this ghost, Timothy McVeigh, executed less than a year before. But surely the nihilism of his act parallels that of

September 11, as does its unpardonable violence. To relate them is to acknowledge the global, rather than domestic, context of political acts. At that moment, this blurring of boundaries was too threatening to be allowed.

When hegemony is under siege, when the imagined political landscape is under attack, there is little tolerance for complexity of meaning. But complexity is just what the diverse multitude in a global public sphere demands. Striking was the speed with which every image taken of the New York City disaster was reduced within a week to one image, the American flag, and under it one caption, "the nation under attack." With brutal simplification, President George W. Bush declared: "you are with us or against us." Hundreds of thousands demonstrating for peace around the globe were simply ignored. Millions of critics of US foreign policy at home and abroad were placed under suspicion.

George W. Bush, well advised after his alarming initial slip of calling for a "crusade" against "cowards," spoke eloquently of the need to make a clear distinction between two Islams: one, a great and honorable religion that has been a humanizing force over the centuries and is practiced in multiple ways by more than a billion people; the other, a subterfuge for criminal acts of terror. Bush has said it: a small group of men must not be allowed to "hijack" the multitude. And who are we, if not this multitude, forced by both sides to acquiesce in the killing of innocent civilians? But to express a cosmopolitan consciousness at that moment was seen as a threat to exclusionary loyalties. We were made to feel afraid.

Terror produces terror, as observers have long noted. Bin Laden and his supporters indeed pose a threat, but that threat doubles when it is countered in kind. A "fundamental paradox" of the paranoid style in American politics, wrote Richard Hofstadter in 1952, the era of the Cold War, "is the imitation of the enemy."[4]

Now, as on that occasion, the acts of enemies reflect each other. The engagements of war cannot exist without this mirroring that ensures an overlapping of the military terrain. In this terrain, we, the hijacked multitude, the vast majority, have been subjected to the common paranoid vision of violence and counter-violence, and prohibited from engaging each other in a common public sphere. The "we" who are Americans, under attack by the terrorists, have been given an ultimatum by our protectors to mute our dissent, rely unquestioningly on our all-too-human leaders, and trust their secretly arrived at determination of our interest. To other nations the United States gives leeway according to the pragmatics of diplomatic policy, but one mandate for all seems non-negotiable: to be against terrorism means to accept the legitimacy of the US deployment of its military power globally to fight terrorists as it alone, secretly, defines them. For Muslims, it is not their right to practice their religion that is at stake. Rather, it is their right to challenge collectively, in Islam's name, the terrorist actions of states: Israeli state terror against the Palestinians or US state terror against Iraqi civilians. But even secular criticism now appears contentious. Samuel Huntington, no radical, has observed that in the Islamic world "images of the West as arrogant, materialistic, repressive, brutal, and decadent are held not only by fundamentalist imams but also by those whom many in the West would consider their natural allies and supporters."[5] It now becomes dangerous for them to say so.

Can I continue to use the term United States here? US policy? US violence? Since September 11, now more than ever, we must maintain a double vision if we are to see clearly. There are two United States of America, and any political analysis – whether from the Left or the Right – that aims at accuracy rather than myth-making must make that distinction. The one United States, of which

I am a voting citizen, is institutionally a democratic republic. It is committed by its constitution to a balance of powers – between local and federal elected officials on the one hand, and among the executive, legislative, and judicial branches on the other. (This balance has been in jeopardy from the moment of George W. Bush's election.) It is a nation founded on principles of freedom – not the shallow freedoms of mass culture mediocrity and consumer choice – but the deeply human, I will say it, *universal* political freedoms of belief, speech, assembly, due process, and equality before the law – equality that has evolved over two hundred years of citizen struggle to mean blindness to sexual and class difference, sexual preference, racial heritage, and ethnic origin, with the goal of affirming and protecting difference in all the individual and collective human senses. I am fiercely loyal to the United States of America that espouses these ideals – ideals in no way the exclusive product of our history, but struggled for widely within the global public sphere. I will give my life to defend both them and the multiplicity of diverse human beings that as fellow citizens and honored guests inhabit my beautiful land – and I will defend them particularly against attempts to drape the persecution of difference with the American flag. But there is another United States over which I have no control, because it is by definition not a democracy, not a republic. I am referring to the national security state that is called into existence with the sovereign pronouncement of a "state of emergency" and that generates a wild zone of power, barbaric and violent, operating without democratic oversight, in order to combat an "enemy" that threatens the existence not merely and not mainly of its citizens, but of its sovereignty. The paradox is that this undemocratic state claims absolute power over the citizens of a free and democratic nation.

My own coming of age politically was the consequence of another September 11, in 1973, when the US government committed criminal acts, including murder, in support of the military coup of General Pinochet in Chile that caused the violent overthrow of Salvador Allende, the legally elected, Marxist President. (To think these two September 11 events simultaneously – to think Kissinger and Pinochet together as criminals against humanity, to think the US School of the Americas together with the al-Qaeda camps in Afghanistan as terrorist training grounds – is precisely what a global public must be capable of doing.) Under the logic of the national security state that has existed formally in the United States since at least 1947, the "national interest" was conflated with that of the "free world"; freedom-loving regimes were by definition pro-American; freedom-fighters were any indigenous groups, no matter how anti-democratic, who with US backing attempted to destroy Leftist social movements throughout the world.

A strong, secular Left existed in every Middle Eastern nation in the 1970s. It supported the Palestinian struggle, in Edward Said's words, as "a liberation ideal, not a provincial movement for muni-cipal self-rule under foreign tutelage. We saw it as an integral unit within the liberation movements of the Third World – secular, democratic, revolutionary."[6] This secular Arab Left pressed for social and economic justice in terms antithetical to US military and economic interests, and it was in this atmosphere that the US national security state nurtured figures like Osama bin Laden, Sadam Hussein (who in 1988 with the knowledge of the Western powers, killed 5,000 people in a poison gas attack on Halabja),[7] and leaders of the Taliban, all of whom would learn well the lessons of the wild zone of power.

The US national security state is a war machine positioned within a geopolitical landscape. It must have a localizable enemy for its powers to appear legitimate; its biggest threat is that the enemy disappears.[8] But given a war, even a Cold War, and now given an ill-defined yet total "war on terrorism," the declared "state of emergency" is justification for suspending the rights and freedoms of citizens. It justifies arresting and holding individuals without due process. It justifies killing and bombing without oversight or accountability. It justifies secrecy, censorship, and a monopoly over the accumulation and dissemination of information. All of these state practices are totalitarian, of course.

In 1927, Stalin in his struggle for power took advantage of an almost hysterical fear in the Soviet Union that the Western powers would invade, declaring: "We have internal enemies. We have external enemies. This, comrades, must not be forgotten for a single moment."[9] The perception of a total threat legitimated the implementation of total, extralegal power both domestically and abroad. The word "terror" is used to describe the execution or imprisonment in the USSR of thousands of party members purged in the 1930s, and we are accustomed to equating this terror with Stalin's name, as if one evil individual were responsible, rather than the logic intrinsic to the whole idea of "terror." But Stalin justified his actions because the *citizenry* felt threatened, a state of mind that is fertile ground for abuses of power. According to one participant: "In the thirties we felt we were at war, at war with the entire world, and we believed that in war you should act like there is a war on."[10] The consequence was that popular support existed for Stalin's regime, precisely because he was not squeamish about rooting out the evil source. The language, the thinking, has begun to sound unpleasantly familiar.

I have argued elsewhere that the unlimited, unmonitored wild zone of power is a potential of every state that claims sovereign power, and with it, a monopoly of the legitimate use of violence.[11] Two consequences follow. The first is that no matter how democratic the constitution of a state regime, as a sovereign state it is always more than a democracy, and consequently a good deal less. The second is that human rights, human freedom, and human justice cannot be exclusive possessions of one nation or one civilization. They must be global rights, or they will not be rights at all.

The problem is not that the West imposes its democratic values on the rest of the world, but that it does so selectively. It is intolerable that rights be applied with a double standard; it is inexcusable to attempt to justify the flagrant opportunism of US or any state policy by calling it respect for cultural diversity. Huntington describes Western duplicity:

> Democracy is promoted but not if it brings Islamic fundamentalists to power; nonproliferation is preached for Iran and Iraq but not for Israel; free trade is the elixir of economic growth but not for agriculture [or steel, it now appears]; human rights are an issue with China but not with Saudi Arabia; aggression against oil-owning Kuwaitis is massively repulsed but not against non-oil-owning Bosnians.[12]

We can add to this list: the killing of innocent civilians in New York City is a terrorist act, but Afghani innocents killed and starving are merely unfortunate; the Taliban's violation of women's rights makes it deserving of destruction, while the Revolutionary Association of Women of Afghanistan is not even mentioned as a necessary component of an anti-Taliban regime. As participants in a global public, we cannot allow ourselves, cynically, to accept such double standards. Humanity is the subject of the global public sphere, not the United States. No individual nation, no partial alliance, can wage war in humanity's name. We, the diverse multitude of humanity, must insist on this as non-negotiable: on this point, "you are with us or against us."

The United States was left dangling as the sole superpower after the fall of the Soviet Union, an absurdity, arguably, once the enemy was gone, but – it is what having hegemony means – that did not end its superpower status. If indeed the Emperor had no clothes, no one in the Empire was letting on. The US still had smart bombs and nuclear stockpiles, Wall Street and Hollywood, and that seemed, for all intents and purposes, to matter. Until now, the US has been able, openly, to shift from the moral high ground to raw self-interest and still prevail.

Until now. We in the vestigal democracy that still calls itself proudly the United States of America have the opportunity, now, to free ourselves from decades of being held hostage by the US national security state that has sullied our reputation and stolen our name. We must ask ourselves: How will we citizens, both civilians and soldiers, benefit from this "unlimited" war on terror, when its continuation is precisely what places our lives and our futures in danger? If the American way of life is going to have to change, let it be for the better. Let us not destroy centuries of democratic gains to save a system that exploits the globe's resources disproportionately and disproportionately reaps its wealth; that treats others with superpower arrogance and uses economic bribes to cripple the potency of the newly emerging, global body politic. If the war is brought to the homeland, let *us* be the ones who wage it – not with terrorist violence whereby the ends justify the means, but with divine violence as Walter Benjamin, a Jew and a Marxist, conceived it: collective political action that is lethal not to human beings, but to the humanly created mythic powers that reign over them.

George W. Bush insists: This is not the Cold War but a new war; the goal is not to defend the free world but, rather, freedom itself ("enduring freedom," as vaguely defined as the war). Yet the military action that George W. Bush calls the "First War of the Twenty-first Century" looks remarkably similar to US military actions in the past. World Wars, the particular insanity of the twentieth century, were struggles for territory. Sovereignty was a geopolitical concept. The enemy was situated within a spatial terrain. In this context, "defending the free world" meant, physically, pushing the enemy out, setting up lines of defense, deportation of sympathizers, pursuits into enemy territory, geographic embargoes – in short, spatial attack and isolation. The overthrow – "destabilization" – of nation-state regimes from within was a clandestine action, best done by indigenous forces, so as not to challenge the terms of legitimation of the sovereign-state system in which wars took place.

In global war, conflict cannot be discretely spatialized, a fact that has enormous implications in terms of the imaginary landscape. Because the "enemy" does not inhabit a clear territorial space, there is nothing geopolitical to attack. The fact that the United States has nonetheless attacked the geopolitical territory of Afghanistan is indicative of its self-contradictory situation. Its superpower strength is still envisioned in traditional military terms. But the new global immanence means that there is no outside, a fact that the terrorists operating on September 11 exploited with brilliant brutality. In contrast, the US is manifesting dinosaur-like symptoms by compulsively repeating its old tactics of massive, military response.

Global immanence has changed the role of the media most especially. In World Wars, the news was directed to distinct audiences. Radio and movie newsreels reported the war unapologetically as "propaganda," editing and interpreting events to rally the home front and demoralize the enemy. But when a global audience makes it impossible to separate home and enemy populations, when the vast majority of human beings who are tuned in can be defined as neither "us" nor "them"; when audiences do not sit in spatially isolated bleachers, there is no way of controlling the propaganda effect. The media, rather than reporting the war, is inextricably entangled within it. It is a deterritorialized weapon among diverse populations, which it can both harm and protect. Again symptomatic of the vulnerability of the United States in these changed conditions is that when global media cannot help but expose as false the stark opposition of good and evil that the government proclaims, its first response is to muzzle the media. Its second is to package and "sell" the US government's version of world events. Under conditions of global immanence, these policies backfire. The US must operate within a global media market that it does not monopolize. There are competing brands. Truth in advertising becomes an issue. When al-Jazeera reaches 35 million viewers, including a growing American domestic audience, the good/evil narrative is challenged and complicated. The dilemma, of course, is that an open media is just what legitimates US violence in the global defense of freedom, so that policy rationale is continuously in danger of undermining itself.

Are we witnessing a US national security state bid to transform itself from an obsolete superpower into a global sovereign power? Such sovereignty would challenge the nation-state system by claiming the monopoly of the legitimate use of violence, launching "police actions" against "criminals" throughout the globe.[13] What, crucially, would be its relation to global capital? In the twentieth century, given the traditional American formula of economic presence and political absence (as opposed to the European formula of direct political imperialism), the Cold War was vital for the legitimacy of US foreign interventions that protected transnational business under the hegemonic banner of protecting the "free world" from communism, capitalism's binary other. In the new situation of global immanence, this strategy no longer makes sense. As a political actor, Osama bin Laden is as imbricated in global capitalism as

Bush is. And he is just as imbricated in global media. Again, his strategy has been to use the most current technology against US hegemonic power. Within the terms of this struggle, the hope that a felicitously reconstituted, "post-modern" sovereignty will come about as a new paradigm of power, as suggested by Hardt and Negri in their recent book *Empire*, now seems clearly overly optimistic.[14]

Would a US-based global sovereignty be capable of becoming the violent arm of global capital? Surely, in the present "state of emergency," the fledgling protest movements against global capital are already feeling the heavy hand of the new security and surveillance. But there is a contradiction that may hinder a US bid for global power, at least in the short run. Global capital cannot exist without the freedom of movement that a global war against terrorism necessarily circumscribes. What does seem likely, and not undesirable, is that global capital will begin to separate itself from the protective shield that American dominance has provided. Not undesirable, because the equation of global capital with Americanization has obfuscated the political situation.

Global capitalism needs to be analyzed with the same double vision, if for different reasons, that we have applied to the US state regime. On the one hand, it is the very foundation of the whole possibility of a global public sphere. On the other, because it thrives on uneven development and the lack of universal rights within that sphere, it continues to be an indefensible system of brutal exploitation of human labor and nature's labor.[15] The true nightmare is that, under the terror produced by a total and unlimited war on terror, a US-led alliance of powers (rather than a potentially more democratic and egalitarian United Nations) will develop in a way that protects the global mobility of capital and its interests, but not that of the multitude and the interests of its public sphere.

Global sovereignty that would attempt to monopolize violence in global capital's defense is a case of reactionary cosmopolitanism, because it lacks a radical sense of social justice. Al-Qaeda and the exclusivity of its fundamentalist struggle is a case of reactionary radicalism, because it lacks a cosmopolitan sense of the public sphere. But when radicalism and cosmopolitanism converge in a global public sphere, when the multitude ceases to be hijacked by either side, when Western hegemony is provincialized within a larger humanity, then terror and counter-terror will have lost their hold. Whether that happens will depend on us.

NOTES

1. For these two important notions, the newness of the global defined by its immanence, and the diversity of global society understood as a "multitude," I am in dialogue with Michael Hardt and Antonio Negri's book *Empire* (Cambridge, Mass. and London: Harvard University Press, 2000).

2. Peter Osborne, *Philosophy in Cultural Theory* (New York and London: Routledge, 2000), p. 35.

3. Joseba Zulaika and William A. Douglass, *Terror and Taboo: The Follies, Fables, and Faces of Terrorism* (New York and London: Routledge, 1996), p. 138.

4. Richard Hofstadter, *The Paranoid Style in American Politics and Other Essays* (New York: Alfred A. Knopf, 1965), p. 32.

5. Samuel P. Huntington, *The Clash of Civilizations and the Remaking of World Order* (New York: Simon & Schuster, 1996), p. 214.

6. Edward Said, *Peace and its Discontents: Essays on Palestine in the Middle East Peace Process*, preface by Christopher Hitchens (New York: Vintage Books, 1996), p. 79.

7. Akbar S. Ahmed, *Postmodernism and Islam: Predicament and Promise* (New York and London: Routledge, 1992), p. 135.

8. I make this argument in Chapter 1 of my book, *Dreamworld and*

Catastrophe: The Passing of Mass Utopia in East and West (Cambridge, Mass. and London: The MIT Press, 2000).

9. Cited in ibid., p. 7.

10. Cited in ibid.

11. Ibid., Chapter 1.

12. Huntington, *The Clash of Civilizations*, p. 184. Huntington, the realist, concludes with a non-argued platitude: "Double standards in practice are the unavoidable price of universal standards of principle." He gives up on the idea of a global public sphere from the start.

13. As US Supreme Court Justice Sandra Day O'Connor observed, the whole question of criminal rights becomes murky in this situation (New York *Times*, September 29, 2001). It is not democratic to the globe to have the global sovereign elected by the US people; it is not democratic to the US people to have its elected President be a global sovereign.

14. Hardt and Negri, *Empire*, p. 139. Hardt and Negri do not face squarely the problem of the legitimate use of violence, which is central to the question of sovereignty.

15. See Teresa Brennan's excellent analysis, *Exhausting Modernity: Grounds for a New Economy* (New York and London: Routledge, 2000).

2. "Postcard of War #13/18. Based on Modern Beirut, International Center of Water-Skiing" (fragment), from *"Wonder Beirut: The Story of a Pyromaniac Photographer"* by Joana Hadjithomas and Khalil Joreige.

3. "Postcard of War #12/18. Based on Beirut: General View with the Mountains" from "*Wonder Beirut: The Story of a Pyromaniac Photographer*" by Joana Hadjithomas and Khalil Joreige.

TWO

CRITICAL THEORY
AND ISLAMISM*

It is with deep respect for my colleagues and friends here today that I speak not about a past theoretical tradition, but about the present historical situation. I am aware that we may not share the same political sensitivities at the moment, sensitivities that run very deep. No one knows the future implications of what is now in process in the world. When it comes to history, we have no predictive science. This is as it should be, because the very concept of history asserts that human beings have agency, hence the possibility that human development is not predetermined – not by nature, nor by God, nor by the totality of history itself.

* This chapter is a revised and expanded version of a talk presented at the conference: "How Does Critical Theory Matter Now?", organized by Professor Helmut Dubiel at New York University, December 7–8, 2001. I am especially grateful for the challenging criticisms of Seyla Benhabib and Saba Mahmood.

41

Freedom, the condition of possibility of history, demands that we act despite imperfect knowledge – without, as Adorno said, a safety net. As critical intellectuals, our role at this moment is to refuse to be intimidated by the so-called majority, to think and write as truthfully as we can in multiple ways, against the grain of the forces that are now riding the tide of history. We have that privilege and that responsibility as a consequence of the division of labor in society. While most working people must accept the given world in order to get on with their daily business (and for tens of thousands that business is now war) intellectuals serve society best by stepping back from the world long enough to question the hegemonic discourses that justify it. This is the essence of all variants of "critical theory." They provide cognitive experience at a level of reflection (let us call it knowledge rather than mere information) that has the power to dispel the illusion of the inevitability of events by demonstrating that it is how we conceive them that gives them their aura of fate.

As one such gesture of critical reflection, I want to speak today about Islam – not its ancient heritage, not its golden medieval times, not its folkloric customs, but its modernity, precisely the modern, politicized Islam that George W. Bush wants to tell us this crisis is "not about." By attempting to silence Islam as a political discourse, by reducing it to a religious practice, Bush is in effect closing off public discussion of how the many varieties of Islamism are challenging and extending the discursive field of political resistance. Such a discussion, however, is there to be engaged within the *global* public sphere, as opposed to our own provincial one, and there is urgency to do so. But this urgent task requires, paradoxically, taking time, the time to read not only news reports and journalistic comments that record and react to the kaleidoscope of daily events, but scholarly articles and books, whole books written by critical theorists like Akbar Ahmed, Leila Ahmed, Mohammed Arkoun,

Talal Asad, Ahmet Davutoglu, Saba Mahmood, Ziba Mir-Hosseini, Abdelwahab El-Messiri, Ali Mirsepassi, Ali Moussalli, Bobby Sayyid, Hisham Sharabi, Azzam Tamimi, Bassam Tibi. These scholars (who in no way speak with one voice) have been trained in the West where many are citizens; most live and teach here.[1] They are fluent in the traditions of Husserl's and Heidegger's phenomenology, Foucault's analyses of power and truth, Gramsci's work on organic intellectuals, Derrida on deconstruction, the radical democracy of Laclau and Mouffe, the cultural studies of the Birmingham school, the postcolonialism of Spivak and Bhabha, and the critical theories of Adorno, Horkheimer, Benjamin, and Habermas. They have been writing for Western audiences for at least the past decade,[2] engaged in the crucial task of making clear how Western phenomena such as secularization, modernization, and nationalism change, not their *conceptual* meaning as they move from the West to non-West, but their material referent, and with it, their political value.

We might, using Adorno's language of non-identity, say that these writers demonstrate how the object (the contextualized referent) does not go into its concept without leaving a remainder: how lived experience escapes the names we attach to it – how, for example, "progress" as actually lived by the Muslim world has not been progressive; how Afghanistan's so-called "backward" condition is precisely an effect of global modernity; how the alliance of Arab regimes with the "democratic" West has worked to repress democracy. These writers place a modern value on what can be called "Islamism," which is to be compared with liberalism, Marxism, nationalism, Pan-Arabism – even post-modernism. Islamism is not a religious discourse, but a political one.[3] It is a debate about modernity, expressed in multiple voices, encompassing varied and conflicting theoretical positions that are meant to have practical, political effects.

Recognizing Islamism as a modern discourse hardly places it beyond criticism. That is not the point. None of these writers are apologists for fundamentalism in its violently terrorist or socially brutal forms, and some are critical even of its moderate manifestations. Their work, rather, demonstrates that because Islamism is not derivative of Western discourse, it raises the political issues of modernity in a different way, one that changes the parameters of the theoretical discussion set by the West. In a sense, the very existence of Islamism displaces the critique of modernity from the Western *cul de sac* of the "totally administered world" that Adorno and Horkheimer deplored as the negative consequence of the dialectic of the European Enlightenment. Engaging in dialogue with this difference gives us the barest glimmer of a possible, not-yet-existing alternative to *both* self-congratulatory scenarios: the distorted economic development that Western hubris posits as the end-goal of history, and the violent destruction that religious extremists sanctify as virtue.

Mediating between critical discourses, the writers named above hold us fast to the true meaning of democracy by demonstrating that Islamist discourse cannot be excluded from the global discussion merely because its premises are non-Western. Their arguments are subtle because they are specific, and I apologize in advance for the inadequate and partial representation of this rich literature in the brief comments that follow. But by critically engaging even a very small part of the discussion of Islamism, I hope to gesture toward the cognitive experience of the non-identical that their theoretical accounts provide.

Modernization has been for the Muslim world a task of cultural submission.[4] This is of course true generally for postcolonial societies, but if we follow the argument of Bobby Sayyid, what distinguishes the Muslim experience is that at its Anatolian center the great modernizer Mustafa Kemal, "father" (*Atatürk*) of the Turkish secular nation, so thoroughly relegated Islam to the dustbin of history that no modern political project could henceforth evoke its name.[5] Kemal insisted on adopting not only the political forms but the cultural signs of the West by secularizing education, outlawing Muslim dress and "uncivilized" headgear, and even inventing a Turkish national opera that mimicked European style.[6] Under the influence of Kemalism, Islam, which for centuries had been for the Muslim world what Sayyid (following Horkheimer) calls its "ideological cement," was "de-sedimented" (Husserl) from the "lifeworld" of ordinary people. Islamic belief, while remaining the matrix of meaning in everyday life, became, schizophrenically, the "constitutive outside" (Derrida) of Turkish national identity, marking its limit, and thereby its extent.[7] As an indigenously produced "Orientalist" (Said) discourse, Kemalism became the lingua franca for secularizing, Westernizing development throughout the Muslim world.

Paradoxically (dialectically?), once Islam was free from traditional institutional arrangements, emptied of any political use yet still widely dispersed within cultural life, it became available for articulations of political resistance to the postcolonial order. As a counter-hegemonic discursive field it became not simply a vehicle through which secular demands of dissatisfied classes were expressed (Sayyid explicitly rejects a Marxist analytical frame), but a "means by which interests and identities [were] formed."[8]

Precisely because it was banned from official discourse, Islam became a "master signifier" (Lacan; Žižek) knitting together the polysemic political debates of opposition within the Muslim world. "Islam is [here Sayyid draws on Richard Rorty] the thinnest of phrases in Muslims' final vocabulary. It is this thinness which makes it difficult to contest. Ultimately, for Muslims, Islam is another word for 'Goodness incarnate.'"[9] Thus, when Islamists claim that the best government is an Islamic government, they are stating a minimal, indeed, tautological truth.

Now, good government is precisely what the Western-oriented states of the Muslim world have insufficiently provided. Kemalist-inspired "secular" rule has too often meant dictatorship, the abrogation of civil liberties, and the violation of human rights. This is not to say that the revolutionary fundamentalist Islamic states have protected such rights. Iran is the prime example. Both the Western-backed Pahlavi monarchy of Iran under Shah Mohammad Reza, and the Revolutionary Republic of Iran under the *faqih* (spiritual guidance) of Ayatollah Ruhalla Khomeini were regimes that practiced state terror.[10] Again, this is not Sayyid's point (although it must be ours). Rather it is to recognize that Iran's Islamist revolution "constituted a new Muslim subjectivity," one that is indisputably modern and just as indisputably non-Western, providing a blow to Kemalism's monopoly of legitimation, and affirming the Islamic daily world in which the majority of the population actually conduct their lives.

What is involved here is not freedom but dignity. And in a postcolonial context, dignity matters. Better put, dignity *is* freedom in a different sense, as liberation from Western hegemony. This is where the "colonial difference" matters:[11] if the adoption of Western-defined freedom brings with it submission to Western power, the purported goal is undermined by the self-alienating means.

But we need to be careful here. It is the intellectually critical and socially accountable power of Islamism that deserves our respect, not its instrumentalized uses by groups in power to garner unquestioning support and to silence internal opposition. The colonial difference is not a license for abuses of power by Islamist regimes.

If Al Banna and Sayyid Qutb of the Muslim Brotherhood were victims of the Egyptian state, this does not justify the Muslim Brotherhood's acquiescence to state terror against Mahmoud Mohamed Taha in Sudan, or the killing of 10,231 individuals of the secular Left by the regime of the Revolutionary Republic of Iran in the early 1980s. State terror does not change its name when it is implemented by clerics.[12]

We are engaging with discourse here, not the violence that silences speech. As a discourse of political opposition, Islam is capable of playing the role that "reason" does in the Western discourse of the Frankfurt School, so that statements such as "the Islam of al-Qaeda, or the Taliban in Afghanistan, or Khomeini in Iran, or Numeiri in the Sudan is un-Islamic" become critically meaningful in ways that calling the same phenomena "backward" or "religiously fanatical" surely does not.[13] Just as in Western critical theory the great defenders of reason are those who criticize the rationalization of society in reason's name, so today's progressive Muslims are able to use Islam as an immanent, critical criterion against its own practice, with similar effect. So long as state regimes that claim not to have abandoned indigenous, Islamic values in fact violate them at every turn, so long as they are composed of corrupt power elites, nominally Muslim but ardently Western-materialist in their personal consumption, catering to foreign interests over domestic needs despite the growing gap between rich and poor, Islamism will continue to have genuine popular appeal.

Islamic feminisms (and they are multiple) can be interpreted in this context. When educated women defy norms by choosing to wear the burqa, they are refusing visual identification with the Westernized elite whom they are expected to join. Far from slipping back to the archaic past, these women may be seen as expressing democratic solidarity with the non-elite Muslim men and women whom the material benefits of modernity Western-style have never reached – at the same time performing their own feminist critique of the culture industry's reification of women's bodies.[14]

When a young Islamist lectures to her religiously ignorant father that "when it was necessary, our prophet undertook his own tasks and helped his wife; he swept the house," she is challenging Muslim patriarchy from within, by its very means of legitimation.[15] As Ibrahim Kaya insists, in the case of Turkey, "veiled women are highly militant political actors," whose appropriation of tradition in defiance of Kemalist norms is producing "a new identity formation" as decisively modern as it is non-Western.[16] This does not justify Islamists dictating from above *the* path for Muslim women; but it does suggest that dictating such a path from outside, according to Western notions, misses an opportunity to expand the discourse of feminism, and also its power.

Ziba Mir-Hosseini's interviews in her native Iran with clerics who hold varying positions on women's rights – from traditionalist to modernist – exposes the vast terrain of discursive struggle that has developed among interpreters of Islam in response to feminist concerns of Iranian women within the Islamic Republic.[17] Saba Mahmood describes her fieldwork in Cairo among women in the mosque movement who have mobilized independently, against the male monopoly of exegetical practice, to teach each other Islamic doctrine, "thereby altering the historically male-centered character of mosques as well as Islamic pedagogy" in their *actions*, even as they uphold as *theory* a discursive tradition that might seem to affirm women's subordination. Their practice leads Mahmood to insist that the "desire for freedom and liberation is a historically situated desire whose motivational force cannot be assumed *a priori*" – hence what constitutes women's agency needs to be thought in expanded terms, and not exclusively according to the Western model.[18] When Leila Ahmed describes from her childhood the experience of two Islams, one of men, official and textual, the other of women, non-dogmatic and customary, she identifies Islamic feminism as a process whereby women sort out the meaning of their lives.[19] The feminist theorist Zillah Eisenstein affirms that the politicization of Muslim women in their struggle for rights is "on their own terms, from their own understandings of what Islam means. They do not need 'the' west for an assist." At the same time, she observes that the separation of gender roles in the present crisis is impossible to deny, as is the negative impact of militarized masculinity on *both* sides.[20]

Feminist solidarities across religious and cultural differences are crucial in the current political struggle, due to the absolute centrality of issues of women and sexuality in the debates. Patriarchy is not, as the old Marxist Left would have it, a secondary contradiction subordinate to class.[21] Islam is not, as the Taliban ruled, a justification for women's inequality, or for the entrenchment of neopatriarchal social forms. But just as certainly: liberation is not, as the Bush regime advertises, a matter of assimilating Muslim women into the truncated agenda of women's rights endorsed by the Republican administration.[22] Eisenstein, whose response to September 11 has been exemplary for feminists, protests with abundant clarity: "It is unforgivable to use women's rights as a pawn in war to rally global forces for war.... [I]t is unconscionable to wrap US bombs in women's rights discourse."[23]

We, as critical theorists, need to make Western audiences aware that Islamism as a political discourse embraces far more than the dogmatic fundamentalism and terrorist violence that dominate in the Western press. It is also a powerful source of critical debate in the struggle against the undemocratic imposition of a new world order by the United States, and against the economic and ecological violence of neo-liberalism, the fundamentalist orthodoxies of which fuel the growing divide between rich and poor. This is to say that secularization is no guarantee against dogmatic beliefs, and that even foundational religious texts are open to multiple interpretations. Islamism has become a site within civil society of social movements that struggle in the most diverse ways to come to grips with the inequities of modern life, which have developed within the period of dominance by the West – a West that for Islamists included the atheistic, materialistic Soviet Union that so faithfully mimicked the model of Western modernization, along with the Western-Orientalist judgment of Islam as an irredeemable obstruction to historical progress.

Since the 1970s, Islamist organizations have proliferated within civil society, providing social services for the community (*umma*) that neither secular nor Muslim governments have delivered. *Jihad* means struggle on three levels, only one of which – a last resort, least pleasing to God – is violent. On the community level, it means to fight with full moral force for economic justice, equality, and social harmony – not only for the nation, but for the entire Islamic world. We can appreciate the supranational appeal of such a pan-Islamic identity, which *could* become the basis not only for political alliances but for a regional economy, eschewing usury and redistributing wealth, reflecting Islam's tenets of social justice, to which today's Muslim financial regimes give little more than lip service. We can also recognize how threatening such an economic union, were it to seriously challenge the orthodoxy of a "free" market, would be to the hegemony of neo-liberalism within the global economy.[24]

Tolerance is an Islamic virtue, based not on a discourse of rights but on one of norms. It is no accident that Jews, expelled from Europe at the beginning of its modern era and violently persecuted at its end, survived in the Ottoman Empire, where, like Christians, they were respected as "people of the Book." Racism is rejected unconditionally by Islamic doctrine (if not practice). At the same time, the extensive sense of community and brotherhood has limits as to what or who will be tolerated, limits that critical theorists cannot possibly defend. "There is no compulsion in religion," states the Qur'an, unequivocally. And yet, in practice, Islamist protection of dissenters and non-believers still falls far short of the genuinely cosmopolitan tolerance that our new, global reality demands. Political pluralism stops short of participation by polytheist or atheist parties, who (with rare exceptions) are harshly excluded; sexual practices are brutally punished if they violate the Qur'an; religious law (*shari'a*) is not open to revision by democratic vote (although critical interpretation – *ijithad* – of the *shari'a* functions very much like Western judicial review, and continues to undergo significant historical transformation). Given the ambiguous record of Islamic regimes now in existence, we must admire the cosmopolitan sophistication of the Indonesian Islamic leader, Abdurrahman Wahid, whose *secular* vision of democracy was *religiously* motivated to protect the rights of Indonesia's religiously diverse populations as is required by the Islamic idea of tolerance. Wahid was strongly influenced by Latin American liberation theology, as was Ali Shariati, whose lectures in the 1970s influenced the more tolerant forces of the Iranian Revolution, and also the Egyptian Islamist and anti-Marxist, Hasan Hanafi, who admired the Western philosophers, Fichte, Spinoza, and Kierkegaard, and whose political positions reflected those of the Muslim Brotherhood during one point in that organization's multiple histories of struggle.

Not all Islamist movements or positions need to be defended in order to acknowledge that Islamism enables political discourses that are modern in their own terms, rather than as a failed mimicry of the West. Within the postcolonial context, this is its critical appeal. The vast discursive terrain of Islamism is a creative space for political articulations of protest against present inequities of power, from which we Western critical theorists have some things to learn – and to which we can fruitfully contribute within a global public sphere, so long as we recognize that even among critics of power, Western hegemony has been problematic.

The dialectic of Enlightenment has morphed out of recognition from its original, post-World War II articulation. The new global context necessarily alters conceptions – even critical ones – that have been definitive for comprehending the modern age. Under these changed conditions, those of us for whom democracy and human rights are fundamental values risk violating those values in attempting to impose them. Democracy means treating people democratically. If we in the West find that under present economic, political, and cultural arrangements of power we cannot do this without danger to our own existence, then the defense of democracy demands not military force, but a radical questioning of these power arrangements.

NOTES

1. At the time of publication of the studies consulted for this chapter, A. Ahmed (from Pakistan) was at the University of Cambridge; L. Ahmed (from Egypt) was at the University of Massachusetts, Amherst; Arkoun (from Algeria) was Professor Emeritus at the Sorbonne; Asad (from Saudi Arabia and Pakistan) was at the University of Chicago; Davutoglu (from Turkey) was at Marmara University, Istanbul; Mahmood (from Pakistan) was at the University of Chicago; Mir-Hosseini (from Iran) was at Cambridge University; El-Messiri (from Egypt) was at Ein Shams University in Cairo; Mirsepassi (from Iran) was at Hampshire College;

Moussalli (from Egypt) was at the American University of Beirut; Sayyid (from Britain) was at the University of Manchester; Sharabi (from Palestine) was at Georgetown University; Tamimi (from Palestine) was Director of the Institute of Islamic Political Thought in London; Tibi (from Syria) was at Göttingen and Harvard Universities.

2. The European context for their work was shaped in part by, in France, the debate over students wearing the veil in public schools, and in England by the Rushdie Affair. Despite (or because of) the American–Iraqi Gulf War, there was much less of a public discussion of Islamism in the US in the 1990s, where ignorance of this intellectual movement is far greater, and with the events of September 11, arguably far more dangerous.

3. Islamism is "theological" in the sense that politics is discussed in a religious idiom, and the difference, particularly, between Sunni and Shi'ite Islam has had repercussions not only for the discourse, but for the politics that emerges from it (most profoundly in the Iran–Iraq War). But Islamist politics increasingly transcends theological splits, centrally in the support for Palestine (by Shi'ites *and* Sunnis, Iran and Iraq).

4. Edward Said's book, *Orientalism* (New York: Pantheon, 1978), is a foundational text for this discussion, as is Bryan S. Turner's *Marx and the End of Orientalism* (London: George Allen and Unwin, 1978) that criticizes the Eurocentricity of the Marxist concept of oriental despotism. On the wider issue of cultural submission in the colonies, see also the work of Spivak, Prakash, Chatterjee, and Chakrabarty on South Asia; the work of Dussel, Mignolo, and Quijano on Latin America, and generally the discussions of postcolonialism and Subaltern Studies, and the work of the Birmingham School.

5. Bobby S. Sayyid, *Fundamental Fear: Eurocentrism and the Emergence of Islamism* (London: Zed Books, 1997), pp. 63–9. Sayyid, a former student of Ernesto Laclau at Birmingham who came of age in the climate of postmodernism, is one of the most diligent in mediating between Islamism and Western theory, which is why I have cited his book here. He is heavily indebted to predecessors, including scholars I have mentioned above. I criticize his conclusions in chapter five, below.

6. Kutlug Ataman (b. Istanbul 1961, studied film in the US, lives and works in London) has produced a brilliant documentary on Semiha Berksoy, the original Turkish opera star, "Semiha B Unplugged" (1997). Humorous and critical, the film is sympathetic to the star's struggle for personal freedom, while satirizing Kemalist Turkey's mimicking of the West.

7. Sayyid, *Fundamental Fear*, pp. 81ff.

8. Ibid., p. 39.

9. Ibid., p. 48.

10. Increasingly in the 1970s, "the shah turned to SAVAK (State Security and Information Agency), his CIA- and MOSSAD (Israeli)-trained secret police to repress the opposition: liberal secular and religious nationalists as well as Marxists. . . . As James Bill has noted, the shah 'abandoned his past policy of balancing coercion with cooptation. . . . The new policy resulted in a reign of terror'" (John L. Esposito and John O. Voll, *Islam and Democracy* [New York and Oxford: Oxford University Press, 1996], p. 55). But the establishment of the Islamic Republic after 1979 did not eliminate state terror, as purges and repressions occurred in the early 1980s and again late in the decade, now in the name of "Islamic justice": "A 'royal reign of terror' was replaced by a 'clerical reign of terror'; only the political actors or players changed, not the practices. Imprisonment, arbitrary trial, torture, censorship, and monitoring by security forces continued. If the notorious and dreaded Evin prison was emptied of its Pahlavi prisoners, it was filled again by those of the Islamic Republic. SAVAK was renamed SAVAMA. . . . Amnesty International reported that, in 1993, 'Political arrests, torture, unfair trials, and summary executions were reported throughout the country'" (ibid., pp. 70–1).

11. This is Walter Mignolo's term for the mediation between historical experiences of (post-)colonial countries and the Western terms used to describe them. See Mignolo, *The Darker Side of the Renaissance: Literacy, Territoriality, and Colonization* (Ann Arbor: The University of Michigan Press, 2000).

12. On the deaths of the secular Left in Iran, see Ali Mirsepassi, *Intellectual Discourse and the Politics of Modernization: Negotiating Modernity in*

Iran (New York and Cambridge: Cambridge University Press, 2000), pp. 159–79. The radically egalitarian Islamist Mahmoud Mohamed Taha was executed in the Sudan on January 20, 1985, having been charged by the regime President Numeiri with apostasy, an allegation to which the Muslim Brotherhood at the time acquiesced.

13. Similarly, when the Teheran Militant Clergy Association affirms that Iran's newly constituted Islamic Republic has "presented a new definition of democracy," then that republic needs to be held accountable in terms of its own constitution – what the Frankfurt School called "immanent criticism" – by arguing that, as observers of revolutionary Iran have noted, the "practice of the regime in a number of areas is not in accord with its own affirmations of freedom and constitutional rights" (Esposito and Voll, *Islam and Democracy*, p. 77).

14. The issue is whether women *choose* the veil, or whether it is imposed (see Miriam Cooke, "Multiple Critique: The Weight of the Veil," *Women Claim Islam: Creating Islamic Feminism through Literature* [New York and London: Routledge, 2001]; also Leila Ahmed, "the Discourse of the Veil," *Women and Gender in Islam: Historical Roots of a Modern Debate* [New Haven: Yale University Press, 1992]). See also Ali Shariati's famous lectures on Muslim women in Iran in the 1970s, trans. and ed. Laleh Bakhtiar, *Shariati on Shariati and the Muslim Woman* [Chicago: Kazi/ ABC International, 1996]).

15. This example is cited in Nilüfer Göle, *The Forbidden Modern: Civilization and Veiling* (Ann Arbor: University of Michigan Press, 1996), p. 104.

16. Ibrahim Kaya, "Modernity and Veiled Women," *European Journal of Social Theory* 3, 2: 195–214, pp. 205 and 208. Kaya is rereading Göle's book (see note 15) and reinterpreting the data it contains.

17. See the insightful and informative study by Ziba Mir-Hosseini, *Islam and Gender: The Religious Debate in Contemporary Iran* (Princeton: Princeton University Press, 1999).

18. Saba Mahmood, "Feminist Theory, Embodiment, and the Docile Agent: Some Reflections on the Egyptian Islamic Revival," *Cultural Anthropology* 16(2): 202–36, pp. 203 and 223. On the issue of Third World feminisms and women's agency, see the seminal text of Chandra Talpade Mohanty, "Cartographies of Struggle: Third World Women

and the Politics of Feminism," in *Third World Women and the Politics of Feminism*, eds Chandra Talpade Mohanty, Ann Russo, and Lourdes Torres (Bloomington: Indiana University Press, 1991).

19. Ahmed, *Women and Gender in Islam.* Her perspective has been seen as dichotomizing women's and men's Islam, dismissing too completely Islamic Family Law as a rigid and quintessentially patriarchal institution; women have also used this law in daily practice to their advantage. (See Annelies Moors, "Debating Islamic Family Law," in *Social History of Women and Gender in the Modern Middle East*, eds Margaret L. Meriwether and Judith E. Tucker [Boulder: Westview Press, 1999], p. 143.)

20. Zillah Eisenstein, "Feminisms in the Aftermath of September 11," *Social Text* 72, 20, 3 (Fall 2002): 79–100.

21. See here the pathbreaking work of Hisham Sharabi, *Neopatriarchy: A Theory of Distorted Change in Arab Society* (New York and Oxford: Oxford University Press, 1988).

22. The Islamic Republic of Iran has provided more reproductive freedom for women than is endorsed by the conservative wing of the US Republican Party. See Esposito and Voll, *Islam and Democracy*, pp. 68 and 85.

23. Zillah Eisenstein, "Not In Our Name," November 29, 2001, unpublished op-ed piece for the New York *Times.* Eisenstein's current writing on feminisms in various cultural–political contexts supports differences in feminist practices while remaining uncompromising in its radical vision of women's equality.

24. Nationalist politics have hindered regional economic unity in the Middle East, despite repeated attempts (see Michael C. Hudson, ed., *Middle East Dilemma: The Politics and Economics of Arab Integration* [New York: Columbia University, 1999]). It would appear to be in the interest of other actors – the United States, the European Union, foreign transnationals – to keep the region fragmented. If economic policy were politicized through Islamism as a transnational force, the effectiveness of these actors in the region would be seriously challenged.

Beirut Souvenir

4. "Postcard of War #13/18" (fragment).

Abdallah Farah is a photographer whose procedure illustrates the difficulty of making images during and after the war. Three periods can be distinguished through the course of his work. In 1964, Abdallah Farah is only 16 years of age when he joins the photography studio of his father, a former assistant of *Dalati and Nohra*. Studio Wahed is located in Bab Idriss in downtown Beirut. In 1968, Studio Wahed receives an order from the Lebanese Tourism Agency for a series of 24 postcards on Beirut, as well as twelve illustrations to be used in the official calendar of 1969. The orders continue in the following years.

The photographs shot over a period of six months for the postcards attempt to reveal the most beautiful tourist sites in Beirut: The city center, the bank district, the cinemas, the souks, the hotels, the beaches, the modern infrastructure, the urban monuments, the city's most important avenues, and so on. Some aerial views were also taken with the assistance of the Ministry of Tourism and the army.

5. "Postcard of war #9/18. Based on Hotel Phoenicia Intercontinental"

The idea behind the project, which was wholeheartedly supported by the prominent hotels, was to expose the city's modernity, its diversity and its richness. The quality of this work was such that it was regularly reprinted (and imitated). We still find reproductions of these postcards on sale today in Beirut's bookshops, even if some of the monuments they depict have disappeared. Abdallah Farah was certainly not the only one who produced postcards, but his work remains among the most distinguished.

After the Civil War breaks out, in the spring of 1976, besieged and invaded by militiamen from different factions, Studio Wahed is destroyed and subsequently burned to the ground. Abdallah succeeds in rescuing some material, a fraction of his negatives including those of the postcards and hundreds of rolls of virgin films, unshot and unexposed.

For some unexplained reason, Farah keeps quiet about embarking on a new venture.

Three years after the war begins and a few months after his father's death, he begins to damage his postcard negatives, burning them little by little – an intentional process of deterioration – as if he is seeking a way to have their state conform to his present. He imitates the destruction of buildings, which are progressively disappearing before his eyes, ravished by bombardment and street battles. In doing so, he inflicts yet another form of destruction. He spends his nights slowly burning his calendar and postcard clichés, making them correspond to his shattered reality.

Through a process, which integrates within it part hazard part accident, these "damaged" images appear like new photographs. Through the traces of fire and light an indexical rapport is recreated.

By the time Abdallah finishes burning all these images, the official peace ending the war is proclaimed in Beirut.

6. "Postcard of War #5/18. Based on St. Georges Hotel"

During the war, often confined to the house or to the bomb shelter, Abdallah Farah seldom goes out (as he himself says he has nothing of the adventurer or the war reporter). During these long years, he mostly photographs the people close to him, his neighbors, and neighboring places. He uses the unshot rolls of film salvaged from his studio; but, short on products, fixatives, and most of all, paper, he is not able to develop his images. The photographed films begin to pile up, waiting for a better day, for a moment when the shelling will stop, and Abdallah would be able to go out. Since and despite the end of the war, he maintains this habit. He doesn't develop his images any more. It suffices just to shoot them. The reels accumulate, without him feeling a need to reveal them. He nonetheless documents precisely each photograph he takes in a small notebook, describing it thoroughly. They are there to be read, leaving an immense space for the imagination. He entitles this work the "invisible image" or the "image in the text." For us, a little obsessed, we see it as a latent image.

From *Wonder Beirut: The Story of a Pyromaniac Photographer and Latent Image* by Joana Hadjithomas and Khalil Joreige.

7. "The Dead" (*Los muertos*) by José Clemente Orozco, 1931, oil on canvas. Museo de Arte Carrillo Gil, Mexico City.

THREE

A GLOBAL COUNTER-CULTURE?*

It can be argued that the global violence initiated by September 11 has had an impact generally on perception and expression – on seeing and speaking; and that for us as practitioners of culture, business as usual has become difficult if not impossible, because the very tools of our trade – language and image – are being appropriated as weapons by all sides. But surely this appropriation is symptomatic of a pervasive crisis in cultural practice that began well before September 11, and of which we are now strikingly aware.

Do not misunderstand me here. It is not the content of the cultural weapons being deployed by the US or al-Qaeda, by Israel or Hamas, that *necessarily* disturbs our work – although politically and ethically we may be deeply troubled by that content; rather, it

---

* Delivered at the Museo de Arte Carrillo Gil, Mexico City, April, 2002.

is something more insidious: not what is said, not what is shown, but *how*. Language – the tool of thought, and image – the tool of cognitive perception, are being appropriated today by discourses of power in a very particular way, one that negates their usefulness for *critical* practices of theory and of art.

It is not easy to make this point, based as it is on a philosophical distinction between ontology (being) and epistemology (knowing) – in a certain sense, between Heidegger and Adorno – and on a further distinction, made by dialectical logic, which involves an inversion of subject and predicate, and which Feuerbach deployed in a socially critical mode. But let me try to use concrete examples rather than philosophical jargon.

We can consider two variants of political discourse, examining the logical claims on which they are based. The first is exemplified in the statement:

1. Because the US does not violate human rights, it is a civilized nation.

This is an *epistemological* description, and it allows for judgments of truth and falsity – truth understood in the modest sense of what is factually the case. It allows for critical theorists – or just plain citizens – to make a compelling argument in protest should a violation of human rights occur, i.e., that knowledge of such a violation robs the legitimacy of the nation to its claim to be civilized. Language here is not compromised. To put the argument in syllogistic form:

a) Civilized nations do not violate human rights.
b) The US does not (or does) violate human rights.
c) Therefore, the US is (or is not) a civilized nation.

But now, look what happens with a seemingly small change in the language structure – the reversal of subject and predicate that involves a dialectical transformation of meaning, turning epistemology into ontology. Here is the second variant:

2. Because the US is a civilized nation, it does not violate human rights.

The implication in this example is that whatever the US does as a nation *by definition* cannot be a violation of human rights – even if the same action done by an uncivilized nation *would* be a violation. Here the truth-claim has left the (epistemological) realm of judgment and moved to the (ontological) realm of identity. To *be* the United States is to *be* civilized (the ontological claim); therefore US actions – no matter what they are – cannot be called *un*civilized. Or, another example: because I am American (the ontological claim), I am ready to die for my country – whatever it does, right or wrong (suspension of judgment, hence of any need for epistemological justification). I die as a consequence of my identity, my very being. Or yet another example: because my struggle is *Jihad*, a Holy struggle, however I struggle – whatever violence I employ – cannot be *un*holy. Another: Imperialism is clearly undemocratic, but Israel *is* a democracy; therefore Israeli occupation of Palestine for 35 years is not imperialist, but, rather, the defense of democracy.

In the ontologically defined terrain, to criticize US state actions is to *be* unpatriotic; to criticize Islamist violence is to *be jahili* (pagan); to criticize the Israeli state is to *be* anti-Semitic. Now this kind of argument, which is increasingly pervasive in political rhetoric today, in fact eliminates the very possibility of critical thinking, without which democratic debate becomes impossible. Its logic is so clearly flawed (and its unprincipled justification of power is so blatant) that one would assume we could all recognize the fallacy easily and not fall into its trap.

If we consider another area of human practice, the world of art, the situation is not as different as might be supposed. But let us not remain on the level of syllogistic logic, where the fallacy is perhaps too easily exposed. It will be productive (if more difficult) to observe this problem within the context of the history of Western art that has defined the legitimating discursive field.

In the modern era in Western culture, art was secularized, no longer connected with ritual, as Walter Benjamin observed, and hence no longer within the domain of metaphysical "truth." At the same time, art assumed a central epistemological role in European modernity. It is not accidental that Kant's Third *Critique*, which deals with aesthetic experience, was a critique of *judgment*. Aesthetics for Kant meant sensory perception, the representation and evaluation of which is subjective, yet claims objective and, indeed, universal validity. The very definition of what art *is* involved making critical judgments about the material world, specifically, judgments of taste regarding beauty, balance, and harmony – all of the vocabulary of traditional art criticism that to us sounds so out of date. I am not suggesting a return to this tradition, which would be not only impossible but undesirable, if only because Kant's project was socially and politically naïve. I am simply observing that in the modern era, the definition of art was first posed in epistemological form, and the discourse presumed the necessity of critical judgments. Collective judgments were institutionalized, so that one could say: Because it is (good) art, it is in the museum.

It was of course Duchamp's famous gesture of placing a urinal on the museum wall that performed a dialectical reversal of subject and predicate: Because it is in the museum, it is art.

A crucial insufficiency of Kantian aesthetics was that its critical epistemology, while acknowledging cultural difference, did not extend to the context in which artworks are made and validated – all of the social practices behind the establishment of collective aesthetic judgments in any culture. Duchamp's practice turned the epistemological question, what is art? (how do we recognize it? how do we value it?) into a mode of social criticism, a *negative* ontology of the state-of-being of the whole legitimating structure of museums. This gesture (which in its socially critical implications parallels Feuerbach's materialist critique of philosophy) forces us, as practitioners of aesthetic judgment, to include the world outside the artwork. It has been the source of a rich tradition of art as institutional critique.

Nonetheless, the epistemologically formulated question – what is art? (what counts as good art? what has value as art?) – did not go away when answers were sought in the social field. Whether one considers the Anthropofagia movement of Tarsila and Andrade in Brazil that exposed the connection between judgments of art and the context of Eurocentrism and imperialism, or the political challenge to artistic practice that owed its inspiration to the Bolshevik revolution; whether one considers the Mexican mural movement that tied art to the cultural project of imagining a nation, or the struggle and victory of Clement Greenberg in setting the discourse of abstract expressionism as *the* legitimate international style; and (especially) when one considers the experimental, boundary-testing approach of conceptualists in the 1960s and 70s – the question "what is art?" was central. The epistemological criterion of judgment remained the basis of artistic practice, and with it, the possibility of aesthetic experience as critique.

There is a real investment made by many of us today in the idea that artistic practice was liberated when judgments of both taste *and* politics ceased to be the criterion for (good) art. But there has been a price, and it is artists who pay it – although the opposite might at first appear to be the case. The contemporary art world values artists, not art. No art objects are necessary. No social or political usefulness is required. Artistic practices have been deregulated. They are strategies chosen by artists themselves as an expression of their individual and uncensored freedom. Artists are iconic embodiments, almost advertisements, for the slogan (if not the reality) of "freedom of speech." I say not the reality, because to a significant degree it is the museum, the curatorial decision, and the biennials that legitimate the artists, and on which they (un-freely) depend.

But let us even accept the ideological level, the advertisement, as true: that artistic freedom exists, but that it has migrated from the artwork to the artist – as the Mexican curator, Cuauhtémoc Medina, recently described the new situation to me. This would seem to be a great victory for the forces of cultural freedom. But artists are thereby put under the enormous pressure of non-pressure. Their apparent power can quickly reverse into its opposite: evidence that the museums and other institutions of the artworld really do not care *what* they do. The institutions of cultural power are not threatened by what the artist creates, so long as it is done within the authorized, artworld space. (Here, the analogy with the "theory-world" would seem to be absolute, as the academic freedom of critical theorists coincides with our lack of influence in public and political debate.)

Museums have had a striking resurgence in the past decade. They are the preferred form of cultural tourism in an age of globalization, where travel means travel to cities. As the new architectural stars of the urban landscape, museums are attractive tourist destinations because visitors do not need language competence to appreciate the offerings (as they do for the theater, for example). And whereas film comes to the traveler, he or she must go to the city in order to experience the institutional settings of "art."

Museums have become hubs for urban redevelopment and centers for entertainment, combining food, music, shopping, and socializing with the economic goals of urban revival. Museum success is judged by numbers of visitors. The museum experience is important – more important – than the aesthetic experience of the artists' practice. It does not matter – indeed, it might be encouraged – that art installations are one-line jokes, that fashion and art fuse into one, that museum shops morph connoisseurs into consumers. Meanwhile, artists, the emblems of freedom, are present in the museum experience in a ghostly fashion, as traces of creative work, as wish-images of non-alienated labor, playing an imaginary role – parallel, perhaps, to that of basketball players whose presence haunts the stores of NIKETOWN.

In short, artistic "freedom" exists in proportion to the artists' irrelevance. Whereas in Dada, meaninglessness was located in the artwork in a way that reflected critically on social meaning itself, now meaninglessness is bestowed upon the artist, whose critical and creative powers are kept isolated from social effect. As Peter Schjeldahl wrote in the *New Yorker* (March 25, 2002) regarding that year's Whitney Biennial: "American art today can be anything except necessary." It is the structure and social function of the artworld that guarantees the meaninglessness of much of artistic practice today. The artworld is a trap. Promising to protect artists' work from the commercial instrumentalization of the culture industry, it absorbs the best, the brightest, the most talented practitioners of visual culture and defuses their critical power, rendering them impotent within the larger public sphere.

Donald Judd's famous statement: "If someone says his work is art, it's art," first enunciated (in 1966) as a critique of cultural conformism, has been neutralized in the present situation: Art *is* what artists do – whereby the ontology of art is reduced to a mere tautology, and the artist's dictatorial power translates into social impotence. Today's art is "free," because it obeys no laws of judgment, taste, or relevance, submitting only to the decisionism of the artist, who can be scandalous, playful, boring, shocking, or whatever – modes of *being* that have no social or cognitive effect. Even "good" art cannot escape trivialization in this insipid environment. Even "political" art is depoliticized, becoming simply another genre of contemporary practice – which has every right to *be*, but not to matter.

This troubling displacement from the epistemologically defined object of art to the ontologically defined being of the "artist" signals the neutralization of artistic protest within a globally commercialized, self-contained and self-absorbed artworld. Artists have adopted various coping strategies to keep critical practice alive. One strategy is for the artist to use her or his socio-ontological identity – as Chicano, as woman, as African-American – as the content of art, and to render aesthetic experience socially critical in this way. Another is to make the artist's corporeal self the site of art, often in ways that are physically painful or abject. A third strategy is performance art, dissolving the artist's *being* into an *action* that disappears. As a consequence of all of these forms, in which the body of the artist is paramount and not the body of the work, the history of contemporary art becomes a biography of practices. "Self-portrait," that once demanded the material, epistemological task of self-recognition, is replaced by various modes of self-exposure.

I have written elsewhere on the gesture of "disappearance" that struck me as symptomatic in the work of the artists of inSITE2000, the San Diego/Tijuana bi-national show that I helped to curate.* The dialectical reversal performed by many of the in-SITE2000 projects was this: Rather than the artist providing public art for the community, the community provided public sanctuary for the artist. Projects like "The Invisible Man" (Carlos Amorales), "Search" (Iñigo Manglano-Ovalle), and "Blind/Hide" (Mark Dion) were manifestations of this thematic of disappearance. The artists seemed to anticipate the post-September 11 brave-new-world of surveillance, which, because it is being constructed by the "free" world (the ontological claim!), is supposedly not a violation of freedom. Artists hijacked the high-tech instruments of surveillance (Jordan Crandall, "Heat Seeking") or diverted the human/canine agents of border patrol (Mauricio Dias and Walter Riedweg, "Mama") and, under cover of rendering the projects impotent by rendering them "art," smuggled into them socially critical content. Several artists designed actions that went unseen by the art-touring public (Mônica Nador in Moclovio Rojas, Diego Gutiérrez's video delivery project, Alberto Caro-Limón's "Children's Park"). In Valeska Soares' "Picturing Paradise," mirrors made the border seem to disappear. Making visible *in*visible conceptual borders, including the border between art display and daily life, marked the video installation of Judith Barry ("border stories, working title, from one side to another") and the sports/art/ballet/performance project of Gustavo Artigas ("The Rules of the Game"). Krzysztof Wodiczko bestowed upon young women maquiladora workers the exhibitionary power of the artist – as Allen McCullum did for amateur painters ("Signs of Imperial Valley"), while Silvia Gruner's video of her own mobile psychotherapy ("Narrow Slot") performed an act of self-silencing by editing out her voice. All of these strategies erased the "artist" as the focus, thereby challenging the onto-

---

* See chapter 4, below.

logical ground of contemporary art. The inSITE2000 artists escaped temporarily from the conditions of being-in-the-artworld, moving into the sheltering hybridity of border communities in a way that defined public art less as an avant-garde than as an underground. The artist-as-fugitive undermined the relationship between artist and public fostered by the marketing strategies of museums. It suggests the possibility of a changed situation of artistic production, indeed, of all cultural production, one that may have a small, but important, chance of success.

Let me give an example from the distant past. In the 1960s and early 70s (the era of Fluxus, graffiti art and feminist art), the texts of Adorno, Horkheimer, Benjamin, the young Marx, and other critical theorists (Feuerbach, for example) were out of print. Still, they circulated widely in Xeroxed pirated editions that were an enormous success without any help from commercial advertising. The same was true of the music of Lennon, Baez, Dylan, and other songwriters, that moved freely along a proliferating circuit of amateur guitar-players. (One might speculate as to the role that Napster might have played, had it been in existence at the time.) Such spontaneous cultural dissemination is proof that there can be readers of theory and receptions of art without marketing departments. I see the possibility of something similar – something even better – emerging today.

Artistic practice might contribute to a general reactivation of social imagination, circulating via the new media's unprecedented power – nothing less than a grass-roots, globally extended, multiply articulated, radically cosmopolitan and critical counter-culture. In it, artists would relinquish their impotent power as residents of the gated community of the artworld in return for social relevance, relating to publics not as their spokespersons, not as ethnographers or advocates who represent to a global artworld the underprivileged and excluded, but as part of a critically creative global context, where aesthetic experience manages to escape not only the artworld, but all "worlds" as disciplinary regimes.

We can do without objects as art, we can do without an artworld, we can do without ontologically designated artists. But we cannot do without aesthetic experience – affective, sensory cognition – that involves making critical judgments about not only cultural forms, but social forms of our being-in-the-world. But if in the present political climate all of the cultural space of the global public sphere becomes subject to appropriation by power, if it is impossible to exist there on terms other than those set down by institutions of cultural control, then this potential has a very slim chance of being realized.

The German composer Karlheinz Stockhausen notoriously commented that the terrorist attack on the World Trade towers in New York City was "the greatest work of art for the whole cosmos. I could not do that. Against that we composers are nothing." In saying so, he opened up a line of discussion that was censored before it could develop. It could lead us, not to an abstract, "artistic" analysis of the images of September 11 – precisely the wrong direction – but to critical reflection on the autonomy of the artist, the impotence of art, and the anaesthetized reception of global images of reality. We might consider the terrorist spectacle as a staging of Heidegger's ontological definition of being human as "being-toward-death" – not as an affirmation of the "truth" of the spectacle, but negatively, as a critique of the primacy of the ontological dimension in thought. We would need to recognize in the terrorist action in New York City a restaging of military telepresence in the Middle East – the killing from a distance that was used by the US military to bomb Iraq in 1991. Whether intended or not, images of the attack on New York mirrored the aesthetic experience of computer games, disaster movies, *and* the US military – except that human beings became "smart bombs," and the viewers in real time had no capacity to interact. The sobering implications of such reflections might lead us to reject essentialist ontology and return to critical epistemology, making judgments regarding visual and textual culture in all its aspects, including the difficult but crucial distinction between the aestheticizing of politics and the politicizing of art, that as Stockhausen's candid statement makes clear, is in danger of disappearance in our time.

8. Mark Dion, *Blind/Hide*, installation, Tijuana River Estuary Reserve, San Diego, project for inSITE2000.

9. Diego Guitérrez, still from video delivery project, *Two Neighborhoods, one in Mexico and one in the United States, a newcomer and his friends*, Colonia Guerrero (Tijuana) and Castle Park (Chula Vista), project for inSITE2000.

10. Jordan Crandall, still from video digital film, *Heatseeking*, project for inSITE2000.

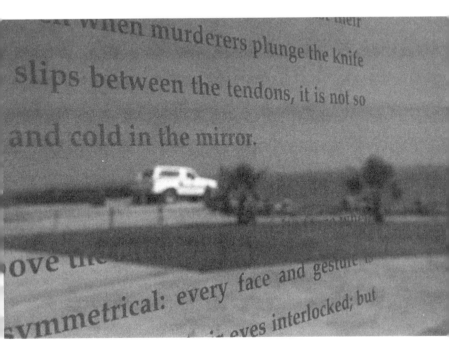

11. Valeska Soares, *Picturing Paradise*, mirrors with text from *Invisible Cities* by Italo Calvino, border, Playas de Tijuana and Border Field State Park, San Diego, project for inSITE2000.

12. Mauricio Dias and Walter Riedweg, still from two-part video installation, *Mama*, San Ysidro border crossing, project for inSITE2000.

13. Judith Barry, stills from video installation, *Border stories working title from one side to another*, downtown San Diego, project for inSITE2000.

FOUR

ART IN THE AGE OF TECHNOLOGICAL SURVEILLANCE

Curatorial Postscript: inSITE2000*

The curator's statement for inSITE2000 was a manifesto. It spoke with bravado about "breaking limits," "transforming knowledge," "redirecting flows," and "disrupting the inertia of everyday life" – words that summoned up the avant-garde for duty.

The artists, who had experienced curatorial enthusiasm before, pretty much ignored our call. We chose as artists highly independent people, which they remained. Offered the freedom to work some-

---

* This chapter was written in March 2002 for the catalogue of inSITE2000, a collaborative bi-national art project that commissioned new works by artists from the Americas for the San Diego/Tijuana region over the period October 2000–February 2001. InSITE2000 was curated by Susan Buck-Morss, Ivo Mesquita, Osvaldo Sánchez, and Sally Yard (see www.insite2000.org).

what off-limits, in a zone relatively secluded from the major routes of global art, they responded with astoundingly diverse projects that took incomparable forms. InSITE2000 produced no new, collective model for public art.

And yet there was a similarity in the artists' ways of working that is visible in retrospect. It had to do with positioning rather than pronouncements. In a surprising number of projects, the artistic gesture was disappearance. Rather than disrupting traffic flows, they joined them; rather than mapping new urban landscapes they blended in; rather than interrupting the syntax of everyday life they sequestered their art within it.

The politics of this gesture is not to confront power, not to criticize commodity culture, not to represent submerged identities, but to move so fully into the social field as to be perceptible for a moment within it – before vanishing in the trans-urban flow.

One is reminded of earthworks that merge with nature and dissolve. Their transient materiality and non-violent relation to the environment are the same. But when artworks disappear within the specificity of a social site, a protective complicity comes into being. Local publics harbor artists as fugitives, aliens (escapees) from the artworld. ■ Lines of flight.

Artworld refugees and public sanctuaries: The society of the spectacle is not unveiled; rather, its veil becomes a cover. ■ Camouflage.

Art, instead of exhibiting itself, hides out in a shopping arcade or a movie theater. ■ Lost in the crowd.

Art insinuates itself into the Friday night wrestling program, or joins up with a museum's wax inhabitants. ■ Shelter.

A shut-down bullfight-ring harbors a radio receiver, pulling alien sounds out of the sky. ■ Nomad sound.

Local youth enact a cover-up for the backboard ball game at the border by appropriating it. ■ Disappearance.

A bird blind in a nature sanctuary becomes a hideout. ■ Camouflaged spectators, camouflaged art.

Nomad-artists find protection in the socius, among other nomads in the urban flows, learning their escape tactics, joining their acts of resistance, boring from within. Art is a sliding moment in the perceptual field between daily ritual and imagination that the public helps to create. ■ Witnesses for the defense.

Some "successful" projects exist as rumor only. Others seek venues secluded from tourist gazes. Children create their art-garden in a backyard that tour buses cannot reach. A video series is privatized, delivered to home mailboxes unannounced. An artist hides out as a housepainter in Maclovio Rojas, where the homes turn into art-works. No one goes to see them. Out of respect for the community. And the artist? ■ Solidarity.

Public art as harboring strangers, an underground more than an avant-garde. Local media as complicit. Pirated band-widths. ■ Invisible cities.

Art that turns the camera on the surveillers. Cameras that unravel the boundary between border patrol and body patrol, (con)fusing voyeurism and police protection, mothering and the law. ■ Resisting arrest.

White cubes that are black boxes. ■ Local hideouts.

An artist undergoes nomad-therapy and videos the trip. In a gesture of self-silence, she edits out her voice. The subject: a hole in the contours of sound. ■ Protection.

The artist framed, caught in the artworld. The artist as fugitive. ■ Escape.

The artworld as a disciplinary order. A truth-regime, the laws of which keep changing, terrorizing its artworkers, whose residence status is temporary. Governmentality: practiced by museums, galleries, universities, journals, conferences, publishing houses. Surveillance: operating through urban renovation and cultural tourism, museum outreach and target publics. Production: powered by curatorial entrepreneurs and the media-critic system. The relentless proliferation of art biennales. Invitations as greencards.

The artworld, ever-expanding, is an anti-market. Artfairs are unfair; competition is rigged. Marketing strategy means market control, curbing the free play of imagination. Media-critics are judges, jury, reporters, all three. Last year's choices are this year's stars. Global extension consumes difference. Otherness as a promotional device: incorporating creative practice at the margins; concentrating commercial power at the center.

The artpublics are smartfans in on the joke, loving the hypes, seeing the sites, playing the game.

Like all global migrants, artists have no job security. They are given no tenure; they have no vote. Solidarity within the labor market is discouraged. Piecework is preferred. Artworld residents are lone individuals, competing to be seen, valued for their power to attract. They are hired to assemble publics, producing spectacles, not art. They provide atmosphere for the barren planet of finance capital. Breath for a sealed bubble. Recycled air.

The time of the artworld is fashion: the new as the always-the-same. The space of the artworld is deterritorialization: no place to hide. The artworld is an imageworld, in which surveillance takes celebrity form, and fame is name-recognition. Artists as branded beings.

And vunerable: The impossible position of advancing one's career while escaping off from its track. Framed: The media-critic system can extinguish the complexities of a lifework with the stroke of a pen, the hit of an icon, an overnight review. Politicians can annihilate whole colonies of artists by a cut in the budget. Morals police are only the most obvious censors. Expulsion from the artworld is a constant threat. Here invisibility means career extinction: Artists are "disappeared."

No wonder, then, that the fugitives try to cover their tracks. Their escape is temporary. They return, global nomads, to the artworld bubble, with media documentation to ensure their re-entry. Lines of flight are reversed. Escape is recoded as a career step, a move toward the next global occasion: a grant, a prize, a biennale – the fast-tracks of the artworld trade.

Interconnected global worlds: An architecture of power. ■ Molar monopolies.

Artworld and theoryworld. Two truth-regimes in global space. Two games on the same playing field. Colliding or collaborating? What chance exists for a theory–art alliance, an insiders' revolt among the players – against the referees? Against the backers? Against the game itself?

Artworld. Theoryworld. Mediaworld. Infoworld. Touristworld. Olympicworld. Foxworld. Bushworld. ■ Oneworld.

The artworld (anyworld) is not a place; it is an ordering system that internalizes truth, a classification procedure for making things known and pinning them down. It sets the conditions of possibility for putting the discourse of art into play. It patrols the borders, ensuring no one will enter – or leave – the discursive space unless preregistered. No exit without a re-entry visa. ■ The rules of the game.

A slice of territory like Tijuana/SanDiego has no such coherence. It is not a world, which is why escape is possible. Contingency leaves its mark on the artists' projects: the way the wind blows a white balloon-cloud, the flight patterns of helicopter patrols over the estuary, the sky-color mirroring Calvino's words, the rain-tears on "La Bola," the faces of the women maquiladora workers. ■ Weather.

In strong projects, escape and refuge are reciprocal: The public, no longer a "target audience," finds a sanctuary in art. ■ Co-nomads, co-creators.

Video shorts, scripted from local narratives and featuring local actors, span multiple show-windows of downtown real estate, saturating the street-corner with cinema-art. ■ Zones of contact.

Amateur artists from a bordertown are brought into the conceptual project of the "professional"; a gallery exhibition features the local mountain they have painted, each is unique. The "professional" specializes in mass production. ■ A world in miniature.

Art takes over high technologies of surveillance and puts them in the hands of those surveilled. Maquiladora workers use art's safe-place in the public sphere to speak the truth to power. ■ Protective exposure.

For nomads traveling along lines of flight, borders can mean safety.

When I was a child (a juvenile-escapee, hiding out in a suburban movie house) the Saturday matinees showed Western heroes as existential loners: outlaws of disciplinary orders, fugitives from the law, heading by horseback to the Mexican border – not critical outsiders still inside, but men-on-the-run, trying to escape before the authorities "disappeared" them. Mexico was freedom. The border was an exit pass. Safe haven. The end of the game: "home-free."

What I am saying here is not about all the projects. It may be contradicted by some of them. I am describing an aspect, an attitude, an after-effect. Art's inconspicuousness, deemed a problem at the time by the organizers, becomes pre-visionary. The artists as clairvoyant, anticipating the brave new world of global surveillance that was born in the aftermath of September 11. This world, the Bushworld, the wholeworld, threatens to leave the independent person no place to hide.

14. Krzysztof Wodiczko, Tijuana Projection, February 23 & 24 2001, Cultural Center, Tijuana, project for inSITE2000.

15. Iftikhar Dadi and Elizabeth Dadi, billboard installation (dimensions variable), 2002.

FIVE

CAN THERE BE A
GLOBAL LEFT?*

How to write for a global public that does not yet exist? We, the multitude who might become that public, cannot yet reach each other across the excluding boundaries of language, beneath the power distortions of global media, against the muffling exclusions of poverty and the disparities in information. We are therefore to be forgiven for relying on the discourses that we possess in common as members of partial publics – religion, national belonging, Western knowledge, global business, ethnic tradition – even if these discourses are exclusive, and punishing to outsiders. It is understandable that we wish our particular discourses to have universal

* This text was delivered at a conference in honor of Professor Hisham Sharabi, Department of History at Georgetown University, Washington, DC, April 22, 2002.

status, although we are aware of the extent to which the appearance of universality is an effect of power. As there has been no free global debate, dominant ideas, even benevolent ones, exist in a social context of domination that affects their truth content irrefutably.

Globalization is not new, but global "immanence" is. I use this term to refer to the fact that in our era of global capital, global production, global labor migrations, and global penetration by technologies of communication, there is no spatial outside, no "other" of peoples, territory or environment against which some of us could conveniently define ourselves and, holding ourselves apart, control our fate. The global space that we inhabit in common is overdetermined, contradictory, and intractably diverse. Our lived experiences are simultaneous and incongruous, resisting division into distinct nationalities, pure ethnicities, or racial differences. We are morally accountable in a multiple world where no religion monopolizes in practice the virtue that would be needed to fight evil in its name, where there is no value-free, objective science that could ground universal, secular truth – just as there is no universal law of the market that can guarantee us a benevolent future.

Those who deny these everyday realities of global immanence fuel fundamentalism, of which there are as many types as there are intolerances. The mark of fundamentalism is not religious belief but dogmatic belief that refuses to interrogate founding texts and excludes the possibility of critical dialogue, dividing humanity absolutely into pre-given categories of the chosen and the expendable, into "us" and "them." And whether this is preached by a head of state, or in a place of worship, or at the IMF, no cultural practice – religious or secular, economic or political, rational or romantic – is immune to fundamentalism's simplifying appeal.

We in the nascent public sphere can do better than to succumb to mythic fundamentalisms of whatever sort. But how do we form a global public? In what language shall we speak to each other, if all languages exclude? How shall we express our solidarity, if communication is culturally contingent? Let us address these very basic issues even if we do not have answers, rather than retreating to the academically safe yet insignificant ground of what can be securely known.

I speak as an intellectual in a Western university context – that is, of course, from a very limited perspective. But perspectivalism does not itself disqualify one as witness to the new global immanence, so long as the glasses one wears are not so ideologically thick as to block out sensory, lived experience – whence comes wisdom, which is by definition neither intolerant nor dogmatic. Wisdom teaches that even if science and religion are infallible, human beings who interpret them are not. But where there is human fallibility – as opposed to fundamentalist fate – there is the hope, the possibility, that we may learn from past mistakes.

Wisdom acknowledges limits, and my contribution here will be a partial and specific one. I will ask: what happens to *critical thinking* in an immanent world? How does global immanence change the conditions of critical reflection, and what significance might this have for a global public sphere? The critical theorists of the Frankfurt School are known for a theoretical method that they called "immanent criticism" (it was the topic of my dissertation, written here at Georgetown University under the tutelage of Professor Hisham Sharabi). Relying on the Hegelian dialectics of negativity, combined with a Kantian humility as to the limits of what can be known, immanent criticism as practiced by Theodor Adorno, Max Horkheimer, and others sought to transcend the untruth of present society in a non-dogmatic, critical, hence negative mode, showing the gap between concept and reality – how, for example, so-called democracies were undemocratic; how mass culture was uncultured;

how Western civilization was barbaric; and, in a classic study, *Dialectic of Enlightenment*, written in the catastrophic context of World War II, how reason, the highest value of European modernity, had become unreason. The politics of this method is radical, not liberal, because it holds ideas accountable for social practice and uses the legitimating values of power against power itself. Its effectiveness has been discovered independently by activists in many political movements. Immanent criticism gave force to Martin Luther King's discourse in the US civil rights movement against segregation, as it did to Mahatma Gandhi's discourse of anticolonialism that used Britain's self-proclaimed "civilized" status against its own colonial practice; just as anticolonial movements generally have used the imperialists' belief in liberty and democracy in order to challenge the legitimacy of imperial rule; just as, more recently, dissidents spoke the truth of socialism to power, undermining the legitimacy of the so-called socialist regimes.

But what happens when immanent criticism operates in an overdetermined, global public sphere where, by definition, the legitimating values of power are not shared? Do the two immanences necessarily cancel each other out, so that immanent critique in one discourse becomes transcendent and affirmative in another? Or is it possible to maintain the critical power of negativity despite the superimposition of discursive frames? And – here is the leap of faith – how might the emergence of a transglobal Left be made possible in the process of critical thinking? What would "the Left" mean in a global public sphere?

To address these questions, let me draw on the concrete case of the Middle East that includes the explosive and urgent issue of Islamism, and on the work of Hisham Sharabi, the man we honor here, whose analyses of Arab intellectual life have been politically courageous, creatively autonomous, and critical. Those who like myself were fortunate to be his students in Western intellectual history will recall his method of teaching the canonical works of Nietzsche, Freud, Weber, Marx, and others. Always he would suggest two entrances to the texts: the first, individual and existential – experiencing personally the attractiveness of the ideas through what he has described as the "subversive and liberating function of reading."[1] The second entrance was social – how the text functioned in a given historical context, how it worked politically to support the inequities of power in society, and how it also might work against these inequities. His understanding of the crucial significance of a double critique, one existential, the other social, emerged, I am sure, from his work as a scholar of Arab intellectual history, and the perspective on Western thinking that such work necessarily entails.

Abdul-Kabir al-Khatibi, the Algerian-born, French-trained sociologist, has written of the necessity of a "double critique" practiced by Arab theorists to criticize their own societies from within, and at the same time to criticize, from without, the Western concepts used to describe them.[2] Edward Said's book *Orientalism* has been, at least in the West, the most widely discussed account of the mythic nature of Western understanding of the Arab world, laying the ground (with others, like Talal Asad) for the argument that Orientalist "science" reveals more about the colonizers than the colonized.[3] More recently, Asad brilliantly criticized Western critiques of the Islamic reaction to Salman Rushdie's novel, *Satanic Verses*, using anthropological methods to describe the curiously specific British cultural reaction to the affair, turning the tables on the former colonizers.[4]

Such literature that criticizes the criticizers warns us, in fact, to qualify the claim with which this essay began: that global immanence is something new in history. Indeed, throughout the modern colonial period, Western hegemony produced global immanence in a one-sided fashion. The immanent superimposition of conflicting values was the contradictory and unavoidable state of the colonized, but not the colonizers, whose very identity as "modern," historically in "advance" of the rest of the world, was their claim to legitimacy as a colonizing force. Other cultures, those of the colonized, existed as objects of anthropological investigation or as "civilizations" accessible to historical study – that is, as vestiges of the past – coeval with but not immanent to "modernity," a word and a concept which, as critics have noted, was in fact Europe's way of defining itself. To "modernize" meant to Westernize, an alien task, in an exemplary case, for "Oriental" subjectivities who, described as inscrutable, irrational, emotional, unscientific, and personalistic, were the quintessential other of Enlightened modern man.

Within the Orientalist context, Arab consciousness was by definition overdetermined: both immanent *and* transcendent, a discourse within the West and a discourse from without. But a critical stance within one discourse did not necessarily include a critical stance in the other. The great Awakening of Arab intellectual life at the turn of the twentieth century employed an "apologist" discourse, justifying Arabic traditions of religious and secular thought precisely because they were compatible with modern Western values of scientific positivism, democratic reasoning, and the rule of law. Kemalism, the modernizing ideology of the Turkish movement of nationalist liberation, broke from Western colonialism by, literally, copying its legal-political and cultural forms. The Turkish leader Mustafa Kemal ridiculed traditional Islam as a "symbol of obscurantism," the "enemy of civilization and science," and "a corpse which poisons our lives."[5] When Western critical discourse was adopted by Arabs in the Marxist mode, this absence of a double critique tended to be just as prevalent, as Arab Marxists were similarly adamant that their own societal and religious forms were vestiges of the feudal past.

Interestingly, it was Islamism that inaugurated an autonomous tradition of immanent critique within the Middle East. The influential Egyptian writer, Sayyid Qutb, a contemporary of the Frankfurt School theorists, critically attacked Islamic regimes as a return of the condition of ignorance – the "*Jahiliyyah*" of pre-Islamic times. Hence present-day Islamic society (Egypt) was un-Islamic. The strategy precisely paralleled the argument of Adorno and Horkheimer in *Dialectic of Enlightenment*, that Western reason, which emerged from myth, had itself turned back into myth. The difference, of course, was Qutb's move to positivity, his affirmation of a return to Islam as stated, literally, in the Qur'an. This affirmation of the true Islam can be seen to mark a definitive break from Western-defined "modernity," allowing for an Islamic model to replace it. But what is interesting about Qutb's understanding of the "self-evidence" of Qur'anic thought, is that it, too, was dependent on the West, in the dialectical sense of critical negation. Islam – the true Islam – appears in Qutb's work as the inverted other of Western modernity: spiritual where the West is materialist; communal where the West is egoistically individual, socially just where the West is greedy and competitive, morally disciplined where the West is negligently libertine. This was, of course, the antithesis of the apologists' strategy of redeeming Islam within the value categories of the West. Redeeming Islam *because* it was "other" opened the way for endorsing an alternative road to modernity, different from both the capitalist West and the Soviet Union[6] – at the enormous price, however, of affirming neo-patriarchal social forms and opening the door for dogmatic, fundamentalist belief.[7]

Now, the Western modernity that Qutb and others attacked was in fact the impoverished tradition of instrumental reason, possessive individualism, and lack of social consciousness that the members of the Frankfurt School and other European Marxists were criticizing from within. It would have taken a radical cosmopolitanism far in advance of what was possible at the time for both sides (German Jewish and Arab Muslim) to join forces in a critique of Western reason in its impoverished, (neo-)liberal, instrumentalized form. But the very thought of such an alliance, an attack launched from both within and without, suggests the power that a new Left in a global public sphere might begin to have today. To accomplish a global critique, however, it is the object criticized that must have priority, not the discursive model. If Western-centrism is to be avoided, Islam-centrism is only its other, not the theoretical solution. But just as clearly from the global perspective, the rejection of Western-centrism does not place a taboo on using the tools of Western thought. On the contrary, it frees the critical tools of the Enlightenment (as well as those of Islam) for original and creative application. To cite the Moroccan historian, Muhammad 'Abid al-Jabiri, who, as a leading critic of Orientalist discourses and Eurocentric world views, nonetheless makes eclectic use of Western concepts from Kant, Freud, Foucault, Marx, and others: "I do not limit myself to the constraints present in the original frameworks, but often utilize them with considerable freedom. . . . We should not consider these concepts molds cast in iron, but tools to be used in each instance in the most productive way. . . ."[8]

If we are interested in the genealogy of a global public sphere, we will need to note that the first *radically cosmopolitan* critique of Western-centric thought did not come to the Islamic world from within. It came from the French-speaking Caribbean, via secular, Marxist transport with a detour to Algeria – and when it appeared it came with a Western wrapping. I am referring to Frantz Fanon's remarkable book, *The Wretched of the Earth*, which (paradoxically introduced by the European Marxist Jean-Paul Sartre) called on the non-Western world to leave Europe "behind" – that is, to produce a modernity that transcended the European model, which had proven itself bankrupt. Fanon's gesture suggested an intellectual liberation of a totally new order because while his politics were still identifiably Marxist, his approach refused submission to any ideology. It resonated with the actually lived experience of much of the colonized world, for whom modernity had meant decline rather than progress – what Aijaz Ahmad has described as "the descent into bourgeois modernity" that marked the era of European imperialism.[9] It received brilliant rearticulation in a 1967 article by the Lebanese poet Ahmad Ali Said (Adonis) – cited as the last sentence of Sharabi's book, *Arab Intellectuals and the West*:

> We no longer believe in Europe. We no longer have faith in its political system or in its philosophies. Worms have eaten into its social structure as they have into . . . its very soul. Europe for us – we backward, ignorant, impoverished people – is a corpse.[10]

Here the very words used by Kemal in rejecting Islam are turned against the postcolonial West. But Adonis is a secular thinker, who has no desire to posit, as did Sayyid Qutb, an inverted West, Islam, as the road to the future. The Fanonist critique was, however, taken up by Islamists, by Ali Shariati, for example, whose thought and writings would play a leading role in the Iranian revolution, and who was influenced as well by the Cuban Marxist, Ché Guevara, and by Latin American liberation theology – an eclectic theoretical mix held together by the object criticized – world imperialism, racism, and class exploitation – rather than any ideological form.[11]

My goal in this short essay is not the retelling of intellectual history. Rather, it is to contribute to a discussion regarding a very specific, very political question: How today, in what intellectually critical idiom, might a global Left learn to speak together? In this context, intellectual history undergoes a transfiguration, no longer a story of specific civilizational continuities, be they Western or Arabic or Islamic, but an "archaeology of knowledge," to use Foucault's term, of a present global possibility. In the language of Walter Benjamin, we are looking for *Urforms* of the present, genealogical lineages that would guide us in articulating a critical discourse adequate to the demands of a global public sphere, in which the hegemony of the colonizing discourses has been shaken so that all criticism must be double critique. At the same time, if a new, global Left is to matter politically, it needs, as Sharabi writes, to "go beyond the negative," rising creatively above critique – without, however, falling into a new dogmatism – a tall order indeed.[12]

We are looking for a route that will connect critical discourses that have evolved in partial contexts, in order to make them useful for a yet-to-be-constituted, global, progressive Left. We will not be satisfied with the realists' maxim: The enemy of my enemy is my friend – as this will not support global solidarity in a meaningful way. We also suspect that the splintering of the Left along the lines of discrete "identities" has run its course as a progressive form of critique, at least in its Western form, where identity politics now threatens to work to the advantage of anti-immigration nativism rather than the protection of cultural minorities. In its Islamist form, "identity politics" is indeed a powerful force, a constituency within civil society of over a billion people, connected in a global network of mosques. But those who desire (or fear) the crafting of this public into a uniform Islamist, global view do a disservice to the richness of debate that informs Islam, which not only allows critical thinking but requires it as a duty. If there are Islamist politicians who think they can count on support from a monolithic, unquestioning Muslim bloc, then these politicians are no less cynical and their motives are no less manipulative than their Western counterparts.

Islamist politics has been multiple and contentious, spanning a wide variety of political positions, including a critical Left. And although the term "Left" is clearly a Western category, emerging in the context of the French Revolution, its non-denominational character may permit it to be applied in a global public space. The "Left" here would mean radical in the critical sense, challenging not only the power inequities of the given world, but also the justifying discourses used to describe it. The Left would also mean cosmopolitan: it would define social justice in a way that excludes no group of humanity from the benefits of, and moral accountability within, the global public sphere.

Given the dominance of the West in recent history, any attempt at global organization risks reinscribing the colonial difference. And yet, as critical Muslims, critical Israelis, critical Americans, Europeans, and others, we cannot allow our identities to hold us apart. We recall Gramsci's insight that hegemony depends not on the absence of oppositional discourses but, rather, on the "disorganization of dissent." We are indeed traveling a difficult road. But let us at least agree to eliminate false steps along the way. I shall discuss a few of these briefly.

There is the view, held by many serious and critical writers, particularly by those from former colonies who may be living in (or writing for) the West, that Samuel Huntington's prediction of a "clash of civilizations" has cleared the way for a counter-hegemonic challenge. Although Huntington, a realist, was describing a gloomy scenario of global struggle, his acknowledgment that civilizations other than the "West" have a role to play in a modernizing project (i.e., that Westernizing and modernizing are not synonymous) posits the coevalness of civilizations that do not have to give up their identities in order to be full participants in "progress." But Huntington is not radically critical in either the immanent or the transcendent sense, and his affirmation of other civilizations is more apparent than real. The Turkish intellectual, Ahmet Davutoglu, speaking specifically to Habermas's claim that modernity is an "unfinished project," asks, then, "who shall complete it? . . . [W]hat will be the role of non-Western civilizations, which have been the object of this project, in the next phase?" Now this might have led Davutoglu to a radical, cosmopolitan position, if he had allied himself with the original impulse of Habermas's statement, its immanent critique of the Enlightenment project that holds Western modernization accountable for its own shortcomings. But instead, Davutoglu drops the burden of double critique and falls into Huntington's fantasy of separate civilizations – as if any "civiliza-tion" could remain separate within the immanent global sphere. The West's self-critique, he asserts, becomes "an inter-civilisational crisis in response to the resistance and revival of the authentic self-perceptions of non-Western civilizations."[13] But a clash of civiliza-tions cannot perform the critical, counter-hegemonic task at hand, which is not to replace one dominating "civilization" by another, but rather, to put an end to the structures of cultural domination.

The recognition of cultural domination as just as important as, and perhaps even as the condition of possibility of, political and economic domination is a true "advance" in our thinking. More-over, if the Western model does *not* have a monopoly on the future's meaning, then we are obliged to look to the discarded cultural pasts in imagining a future that is "not-yet." But – this is crucial – it is to the cultural imaginaries of past civilizations that we must look for inspiration, not the power realities. In other words, cultures must be understood as always radical, in the sense that they are always negotiations between the real and the ideal, hence at least potentially in protest against the societies and power structures in which they emerge. The cultures that defenders of tradition look back to with such nostalgia are the dream-form of the societies that gave them birth. Precisely for that reason, in their time they functioned ideologically, covering up the inequities and iniquities of minority rule, patriarchal domination, class domination – all forms of the violence of power that deserve to be called "barbaric."

Culture *and* barbarism – the barbarism of power that at the same time provides the control, the "law and order," that allows culture to flourish – these are the two sides of the Golden Age of every "civilization," whether it is called the Pax Romana, or Pax Britannica, or Pax Americana, or the Classical Age of Islam, or the heights of civilization of the Aztecs and Incas. No great "civilization" has been free of this contradiction. This was the tremendous insight of Walter Benjamin when he insisted:

> Whoever has emerged victorious participates to this day in the triumphal procession in which the present rulers step over those who are lying prostrate. . . . There is no document of civilization which is not at the same time a document of barbarism.[14]

In revering and desiring within changed current conditions to salvage our different cultural traditions (and Marxism is one of them, as is Islam's Golden Age *and* the European Enlightenment) we would be well advised not to confuse the dream of the past with its reality. As we value the former, we must continue to criticize the latter. Such redemption of past culture would rip it out of its ideological role of justifying not only past violence, but new violence committed in its name.

The goal of a radical cosmopolitan Left cannot be reduced to the minimalist project of changing the religion, or skin color, or ethnicity of the exploiters. Whenever a social system produces a wealthy and powerful few on the backs of the many, a culture worth defending cannot be identified with its justification. Confucianism and Islam may point to the development of a different kind of capitalism, but it is not enough if this "difference" remains at the level of ideological justification, while the exploitation of human beings' creative labor and nature's creative labor remains the foundation of the production of social wealth. What is needed, as Sharabi writes, is not theological exegesis, but critical analysis that might actually solve the problems.[15]

A deceptively attractive argument heard today in some postmodern circles appears precisely not to drop a double-critique, but rather retains them both, knitting two opposing critiques together, Islamism and postmodernism. Now these may sound like highly unlikely ideological bedfellows, but in his intellectually smart book *Fundamental Fear*, Bobby Sayyid describes the emergence of the Islamist discourse of the Ayatollah Ruhulla Khomeini with the aid of post-modern categories gleaned from Lacan, Derrida, and Rorty that almost convince us of the postmodern correctness of Khomeinian theory. Khomeini, he argues, by not even trying to justify his political theory in the categories of Western thought, has managed a triumphal escape from Western hegemony. Khomeini's Islamism has managed to "decenter" the West,[16] leading Sayyid to the paradoxical conclusion: Only by refusing dialogue can true dialogue be found.

This is not a convincing proposal. Critical judgment does not end with liberation from Western thought models. It only begins there. Without denying the positive elements of the Iranian revolution that rejected the Pahlavi Shah's terroristic regime, with its political and military dependency on US government support, we do not need to endorse the violently authoritarian, punishing, neopatriarchal aspects of the Iranian Revolution – which has had significant critics from within the discourse of Islamism – any more than a definitive critique of capitalism demands uncritically embracing the socialism of Stalin. That fallacy was precisely what Adorno and Horkheimer were criticizing when they wrote *The Dialectic of Enlightenment* against both variants, capitalist and socialist, of so-called Western reason.

So the lineages are complicated ones, and Sayyid does his important topic no favors by ignoring the complications. What I am suggesting here is that a truly global public sphere might liberate thinking so that we are not compelled to take sides – "us" v. "them" – or limit ourselves to one paradigm of thought – religious or secular, post-modern or modern – in a way that stunts our capacity for critical judgments, leads to false intellectual and political conclusions, and prevents us from identifying similarities among fundamentalist positions – which must include the self-understanding of the United States as the "Chosen Nation" and the neo-liberal fundamentalism that leads to blind faith in the market mechanism, to name only two of the most blatant, non-Islamic examples. American hegemony is constitutive of the fundamentalist Islamism that opposes it; US and Israeli state terror is not only the effect but also the cause of the terror that resists it. These are the truths that need to be insisted upon by a global Left.

One way that we as intellectuals can help to make such a discourse possible is to teach and write against the disciplinary boundaries that enforce the myth of civilizations as the "difference" that matters. We can make use of critical tools of thought wherever we find them. My graduate training at Georgetown University in the 1970s was impoverished by the fact that, as a European history major and as a student of critical theory, I was not required to take a course from Professor Sharabi in Arab intellectual history. But if civilizational divisions were unavoidable in the second half of the twentieth century, they must not be so today. Hisham Sharabi's critical legacy, both inside and outside the West, both inside and outside the Arab world, opens up the space of a global public sphere in which a radical, cosmopolitan Left might find a home.

NOTES

1. Hisham Sharabi, *Neopatriarchy: A Theory of Distorted Change in Arab Society* (New York and Oxford: Oxford University Press, 1988), p. 87.
2. Hisham Sharabi, "The Scholarly Point of View: Politics, Perspective, Paradigm," in Hisham Sharabi, ed., *Theory, Politics and the Arab World* (New York and London: Routledge, 1990), pp. 36–7. Sharabi points out that Khatibi's French-language texts needed to be translated into Arabic (in 1980).
3. Edward W. Said, *Orientalism* (New York: Pantheon Books, 1978); Talal Asad, ed., *Anthropology and the Colonial Encounter* [1978] (Amherst, N.Y.: Humanity Books, 1998).
4. Talal Asad, *Genealogies of Religion: Discipline and Reasons of Power in Christianity and Islam* (Baltimore and London: The Johns Hopkins University Press, 1993), Chapters 7 and 8.
5. Mustafa Kemal, cited in Bobby S. Sayyid, *A Fundamental Fear: Eurocentrism and the Emergence of Islamism* (London: Zed Books, 1997), p. 65.
6. In regard to the prominent theme of social justice in Qutb's writings, Olivier Roy claims "it is Marxism that is the mirror and foil of the Islamist effort" (cited in Roxanne L. Euben, *Enemy in the Mirror: Islamic Fundamentalism and the Limits of Modern Rationalism, A Work of Comparative Political Theory* [Princeton: Princeton University Press, 1999], p. 81). Euben's book, a landmark in comparative political philosophy, considers the similarities between the critiques of Qutb and the Frankfurt School.
7. Qutb did not neglect a double-critique. A chapter of his book, *Islam*

and Universal Peace, dealing with the hypocrisy of United States policies in the Middle East was deleted by the government of Egypt after the 1952 revolution (Euben, *Enemy in the Mirror*, p. 186n).

8. From *The Contemporary Arab Discourse* (in Arabic), 1982, cited in Sharabi, "The Scholarly Point of View," p. 27.

9. Aijaz Ahmad, *In the Mirror of Urdu: Recompositions of Nation and Community 1947–1965* (Rashtrapati Nivas, Shimla, 1993), p. 20.

10. Hisham Sharabi, *Arab Intellectuals and the West: The Formative Years, 1875–1914* (Baltimore: The Johns Hopkins University Press, 1970), p. 136.

11. "Come friends let us abandon Europe; let us cease this nauseating, apish imitation of Europe. Let us leave behind this Europe that always speaks of humanity, but destroys human beings wherever it finds them" (Shariati, cited in John L. Esposito and John O. Voll, *Islam and Democracy* [New York and Oxford: Oxford University Press, 1996], p. 59).

12. Sharabi, *Neopatriarchy*, p. 120.

13. Ahmet Davutoglu, "Philosophical and Institutional Dimensions of Secularization: A Comparative Analysis," John L. Esposito and Azzam Tamimi, eds, *Islam and Secularism in the Middle East* (New York: New York University Press, 2000), p. 174.

14. Walter Benjamin, "Theses on the Philosophy of History," in *Illuminations*, ed. Hannah Arendt, trans. Harry Zohn (New York: Schocken Books, 1968), p. 256.

15. Sharabi, *Neopatriarchy*, pp. 140–41.

16. "In contrast [to the earlier Islamic 'apologists'], . . . Khomeini does not try to claim that Islam is 'real democracy,' or that Islam anticipates socialism, or that Islam is compatible with science, etc." (Sayyid, *Fundamental Fear*, p. 113).

16 and 17. "Women of the Ruins" (*Trümmerfrauen*), Berlin, 1945, who cleaned and stacked the stones of the war-destroyed city, one by one.

SIX

INTERVIEW:
SUSAN BUCK-MORSS,
LAURA MULVEY AND
MARQ SMITH

(*Journal of Visual Culture**)

JVC: Towards the beginning of *Dreamworld and Catastrophe* [2000] you say that this most recent book is an "experiment in visual culture." It attempts, you go on to propose, to use "images as philosophy" by presenting, both literally and metaphorically, a way of seeing the past that challenges common conceptions as to what this last [the twentieth] century was all about. Would you tell us more about what lies behind this adventurous endeavor? It certainly seems to be a similarly intricate task as the one you set yourself in your previous book, *The Dialectics of Seeing* [1989]. Are such experiments born of a montage mentality, of a Benjaminian

* Excerpts from an interview with Laura Mulvey and Marquard Smith for the *Journal of Visual Culture*, London, October 28, 2001. The full interview was published in in vol. 1 no. 3, December 2002: 325–40.

mentality, or is there something else going on as well? Is there perhaps something specifically Buck-Morssian about it?

SBM: Often I begin simply being fascinated with an image, particularly an image that doesn't seem to fit, or that disturbs conventional understanding. There are 140 images in *Dreamworld and Catastrophe*, and they are from many different genres. Some are paintings, some are photographs or film stills, some are clippings from newspapers – all kinds of visual data. They were the inspiration for the writing of the text, rather than being illustrations of the text, which would not have been written if the images had not been found. That is important to me. It leads to plundering film studies, art history, photography books, and whatever else I can get my hands on. I plunder visual culture for a certain theoretical use.

Benjamin worked that way too, more than we realize. Although he includes very few images in his work, many of his most insightful theoretical contributions are reflections on visual culture. My presentation differs in its dependence on images mounted directly in the text. The juxtaposition of images and text is meant to produce a cognitive experience in readers, who can *see* the theoretical point in a certain way, one that surprises and illuminates. Affect, as much as reason, is mobilized. . . .

Critical Archaeologies of Globalization

JVC: The question is: what kind of material allows us to rescue the utopian hopes of Modernity – as a Leftist project? You talk about rubble in *Dreamworld and Catastrophe*, which is very much a book about visual culture. So what kind of residue, historical and visual, might we address to take this utopian project seriously?

SBM: The project of the Constructivists, for one example, particularly their quite serious attempts to create "socialist objects," industrial-aesthetic products that would be "comrades" of people in their daily life, avoiding the fetish character of bourgeois commodities. Then there is the dreamworld of Soviet cinema. I refer in the book to the movie, *Circus*, directed by Gregorii Alexandrov (who worked with Eisenstein in the 1920s), but I hadn't had a chance to view it until more recently. It is absolutely extraordinary, not only for the Busby Berkeley lookalike musical finale, but for the enlightened way that race is handled, mixed marriages, the whole gamut. It was released in 1936! You don't find racial integration thematized so progressively in the *West* in the mid-thirties.

"Residues" useful for a utopian project in our own time can also be facts that challenge our entrenched Cold-War imaginaries of East v. West, by showing that the cultural connections were more fluid than is generally supposed. In the book I put together a story, a coherent story, from pieces found in disparate places – the fact that US engineers built the factories of Stalin's first Five Year Plan, and the fact that the US public has a National Gallery of Art in Washington DC. How do these facts fit together? Stalin needed hard currency to pay the engineers, and he got it by selling – secretly – European masterpieces from the Hermitage museum to the US Secretary of the Treasury Andrew Mellon, who to avoid prosecution for tax evasion, willed to the government both the paintings and money to build a museum. So the US got "socialized art" – the National Gallery – and the USSR got capitalist steel mills from the Mellon family fortune! I found the first part of this story in the literature of an extreme right-wing think-tank; I found the second part in the art history library. But no one had put them together. The images for this section include photographs of Magnitogorsk taken by Margaret Bourke-White, who traveled to the USSR in the 1930s.

The goal is not to tell a newly definitive history. The pieces can be pulled apart and put together to express another idea. But the constellations are not arbitrary. The ideas they create are not fictional. To move these pieces of the past around is a bit of a gesture of *Der Grübler*, the figure of allegory who tries to piece together what past history has split apart. And the politically utopian interest in these historical fragments comes from the fact that they are all we've got! Where else but to the past can you look if you give up the myth of marching joyously forward, counting on the inevitability of progress? So the rescue of history is not out of nostalgia for the past, but to make the past useful. Really useful. Useful for thinking on the Left today.

The problem with using historical facts is that people want you to weight them in a way that tells history "as it actually was." The book has been criticized for not putting enough emphasis on the horrors of the Soviet situation – Stalin's mass murders, or the disasters of peasant collectivization. But remembering the victims is not a sufficient strategy for the Left today, particularly if recollecting these horrors is used as a way of discrediting the tradition of socialism in its entirety. For us, it is the Cold-War telling of history that needs to be brushed against the grain. My strategy is a pragmatics of time that avoids chronology in order to place historical fragments in useful juxtaposition. I really have in mind as a model the method of photomontage, the political photomontages of John Heartfield and others.

JVC: So this is the way in which the piece you published recently in *Critical Inquiry* on Hegel and Haiti works, for instance?*

* Susan Buck-Morss, *Critical Inquiry*, 26, 4 (Summer 2000): 821–65.

SBM: Absolutely. It's the same method. Thank you for seeing that. After *Dreamworld and Catastrophe* appeared, people tended to conclude that I "do" Soviet Studies. But then I tell them I just wrote on Hegel and Haiti, and they protest. "You're not supposed to hop about like that." Obviously you can be accused of dilettantism here [laughter]. But the method is the same. In both cases I am putting together fragments of the past with the political intent of transforming our historical imaginaries. With the Hegel and Haiti project, it was a task of restoration, putting the historical facts together to restore a picture that the splicing of the story by different disciplines – philosophy, Caribbean studies, French Revolutionary history, art history, print media history – had obscured and made impossible to see.

JVC: To clarify, and without wanting to simplify too much, the article on Hegel and Haiti concerns how, historically, Hegel began to develop a particular model of history at a particular historical moment, and how this model, this account, becomes a guiding principle in understanding the emergence of Modernity. But it is more than this, because you shift the story very far away from its more familiar iconographical, historical, cultural, and geographical milieu, and pivot it through *Haiti* to show not only that Hegel's philosophy of history has a concrete historical whereabouts but also that the master–slave dialectic is very much always already a question of and for the postcolonial, as well as a question of class. What part, then, does the Hegel and Haiti configuration play in the beginnings of your new project, a cultural genealogy of globalization?

SBM: *Dreamworld and Catastrophe* is about the end of the modernist landscape of East versus West. The disintegration of this geopolitical map is, let's say, the end of Modernity – or, better put, a certain kind of Modernity, one monopolized by the West. So now, if you go back to the beginning of the modern era, you have to think *without* the map that is now destroyed. You're thinking back into the space of the origins of Modernity, without presuming that it is going to end up with the Cold-War map that you know. That frees you for other kinds of intellectual projects. So for me it was absolutely logical to move to Hegel and Haiti, as key to a genealogical mapping of the origins of globalization, and of movements that are resisting it in its present form. Our new reality, unlike Modernity, is not inherently Eurocentric.

Basically, the project hinges on an archival find that I would not have looked for if I hadn't already had a hunch that it must be there. That is, the first mention of the master–slave dialectic by Hegel was in the Jena manuscripts of 1803–5; these notes immediately preceded the writing of the *Phenomenology of Mind*. 1803 was the year Napoleon arrested Toussaint-Louverture, who had liberated the slaves of Saint-Domingue and forced the French Revolutionary government to abolish slavery throughout the colonies. In 1804–5, Dessalines took up the struggle in Saint-Domingue, and succeeded in liberating the colony, establishing the "Black Empire" of Haiti. Hegel formulated the master–slave dialectic in precisely these years. So I thought there must be a connection, although academics in the specific disciplines hadn't seen it. Only one scholar, a philosopher from West Africa living in Paris named Pierre Franklin-Tavares, has speculated about a connection.

And it turns out – this was the archival find – that *the* leading political journal in Germany at the time, by the name of *Minerva* – which Hegel read, we know that – had in 1803, 1804, and 1805 hundreds of pages on the Haitian revolution, telling the whole story of ten years of struggle against slavery and colonialism. In fact, every press in Europe was full of the story (except in France, where Napoleon censored the news from the colony). Wordsworth, who was born in the same year as Hegel, wrote a sonnet to Toussaint-Louverture that was published in the *Morning Post* in 1803. The significance of the Haitian revolution for literate Europeans was that "freedom from slavery," the root metaphor of European political philosophy in Hobbes, Locke, and Rousseau, was suddenly shown to be no longer merely a metaphor, but an actual event in world history, and this is precisely what inspired the young Hegel. The inner-historical approach to political philosophy in Hegel's dialectic of master and slave replaced the "state of nature" narrative as justification of freedom. Hegel made a note to himself: "Robinson Crusoe *and* Friday" – in the "state of nature," the slave was already there, *with* Crusoe. So if you just shift the whole story geographically off center, it becomes clear how our disciplinary boundaries and the Eurocentrism underlying them have made that original connection, evident to everyone at the time, impossible for *us* to see.

Now, that's where visual culture comes in. The presence of Blacks in Europe is documented repeatedly in paintings of the seventeenth and eighteenth centuries. What has been invisible in textual history becomes visible in images, including the illustrated books on Haiti at the time, and in the iconography of freemasonry that extends from Haitian vodou symbolism to the watermarks on Hegel's writing paper!

JVC: Surely this conjuncture (Hegel and Haiti) is something that emerges out of a European intellectual engagement with the problem of colonial slavery? Eurocentricism? I'm often not quite sure what it means exactly. Britain, for example, was an Imperial country that also had a tradition of Leftism, even liberalism, which has often been forced into existence by Imperial politics about liberation struggles, questions of colonialism . . .

SBM: Yes, but the story of colonial liberation still keeps Europe in the center, whereas work by, for instance, Linebaugh and Rediker – *The Many-Headed Hydra* – tells a very different story. "Hegel and Haiti" put me in contact with scholars from multiple disciplines, who are doing what I would call a genealogy, or a critical archaeology of globalization. In other words, it is global history, but not in the triumphalist mode that leads to an affirmation of the present global arrangements of power. Rather, the project charts the kinds of resistance that existed historically in the margins, in a space that was not nationally defined. If you look at Haitian history as a national story, it's a disaster, a classic case of failed development and political dictatorship under the influence of foreign capital and the US government. But if you look at the impact of Haiti's slave revolution on Latin America, or how it frightened the slave-owners in the United States, or how the Polish viewed the events there as well as other Europeans, not only Hegel, the impact is enormous. So it is not just another struggle for colonial liberation. It's a global story, one of radical cosmopolitanism, in which Enlightenment thought is already in protest against European hegemony. It has a different valence than thinking in terms of colonies against the mother country.

JVC: Historians here in the UK have recently been pointing out that there is a history that starts in the colonies and then impacts on the mother country. It cuts both ways. In many cases there would have been radical reform movements that would have also necessarily been, if not anti-Imperialist as such, certainly forced to consider British power inside the country as part and parcel of its Imperial status. [. . .]

SBM: You are right, of course. The Putney Debates are an excellent example of what you are saying, and they figure centrally in Linebaugh and Rediker's book. But if you look at, say, Robin Blackburn's book, *The Overthrow of Colonial Slavery*, it ends up being a story about how the support, let's say, inside Britain or the United States for the Haitians played into the Abolition Movement. But that's still a European story. C.L.R. James' classic work, *Black Jacobins*, is still a book about how Haiti was having a *French* revolution. The title of the book tells you that. In moving away from Europe, I was brought into contact with the work of people like Linebaugh and Rediker – and Walter Mignolo, author of *The Darker Side of the Renaissance*, and also Joan Dayan, whose book *Haiti, History and the Gods* examines vodou as a *modern* philosophy. Sibylle Fischer has just finished an extraordinary manuscript, *Modernity Disavowed*, that insists on the centrality of Haiti for the modern history of liberation. A decade ago, Paul Gilroy's *Black Atlantic* initiated this decentering of the historical discussion. He was one of the first to replot the territory of the globe and tell its history in a way that does not privilege nation-states, or national liberation movements. All of these books can be said to be examples of an archaeology of knowledge. They are genealogies of the *urforms* of global resistance.

JVC: To pick up on the issue of maps, and the geography of East and West in particular, we have a cultural geography or topography-type question. Picking up on discussions in *Dreamworld and Catastrophe* again, we're interested to know if changes in the global landscape, both literal and metaphorical, make continuing to think about East and West redundant. How valuable is it to still be able to think about East and West as locatable, as mappable, as articulatable through the directions of visual mapping?

SBM: I don't believe that geography lines up with politics, not today, and probably never. There is no space today where the Left has a home, not even Cuba or China, where lack of democracy corrupts the socialist goals. A real problem for the Left is the fact that there is no geographical base outside of global capital – although Cuba is courageously attempting to enter the global economy on altered terms. The Soviet Union played an important role because even when the Left was strongly anti-Soviet, the very existence of the "East" was evidence that capitalism was not some sort of natural phenomenon that emerged necessarily out of industrial civilization. This bifurcation of Modernity, East v. West, also made possible progressive politics on a global level – Left-international support for the Republic in the Spanish Civil War, to name just one example.

JVC: I think about the changing colors of maps. And watching the geographical transformation over the last twelve years or so, they've been quite profound as a visual experience. To understand where boundaries lie, is to recognize how the world begins to redefine itself from, say, East and West to North and South. For example, the US looks south towards Mexico, not east towards the former Soviet Union. The formulation of the East and the West as a geographical metaphorics seems very much of the Cold War, very European even. The East–West doesn't exist in the same kind of way, doesn't signify as demandingly or as singularly as it once did. So, really, it's a question of trying to imagine what a map looks like when it starts changing. There are some great maps, of Australian origin for instance, that have Australia center-stage, and the other way up. And that's exactly the way the world is from an Australian's point of view! Maps generally seem to reflect and affirm our Eurocentrism. But as the centers of power, interest, and significant activity shift, it's imperative that we learn how the world works through an alternative set of co-ordinates that were always already in place, and were already mappable, but somehow simply not registered by the majority of us.

SBM: Seeing the globe from the perspective of Haiti is liberating in that it makes the familiar appear strange. Haiti is particular, but not unique in the way that it opens up new perspectives. It is not just re-mapping per se, not just that East–West maps are being replaced by North–South co-ordinates, but rather that there is a real effort to visualize the globe without a center. It is very exciting, but it is also problematic from a political point of view. Hardt and Negri's book *Empire* makes the important point that contemporary globalization means immanence: there is no place outside of "Empire's" political and economic reach. But it also means that resistance cannot remain local, or even national, much less nationalist. Even anti-globalization movements have to work on a global level today. That is the challenge for the Left in the twenty-first century.

Politics, History, Utopia

JVC [Smith]: Let's return to the question of time that we touched upon earlier. In *Dreamworld and Catastrophe*, particularly Section II, entitled "Dreamworlds of History," you discuss the crisis of history, the question of how "history has failed us." We're hoping you could say a little bit more about this failure of history, as it shows itself to be a question about the perception of time. Rather than being interested in how history has failed as such, we'd like to know how you conceptualize the problem of reading back against history. (And not just in a Benjaminian sense.) In light of this, and your way of looking back across the concept of progress, do you, perhaps, believe there will be a moment when the Left is going to have to think in terms of a past rather than a future? In addition, different configurations of time emerge across *Dreamworld and Catastrophe*. You talk about revolutionary time, and debates around the end of history – from Alexandre Kojève to Francis Fukuyama's *The End of History and the Last Man*, and so on. And then of course you talk about global time. How do these three modalities of time interact with one another?

JVC [Mulvey]: It seems to me that you are also drawing attention to the idea of a perceived crisis in history – the conjunction of the success of neo-liberalism with the collapse of the former Soviet Union is produced by the success of a Right-wing political and economic agenda. So that if we accept that "history" has been divided across these crises, isn't it perhaps the case that intellectuals, however much these crises might exist, must find ways of knitting the lost continuities of the Left back across them?

SBM: If the utopian dreamworlds of the twentieth century are shattered, if cynicism now dominates political thinking, then we on the Left need to work for a kind of restitution. If fragmentation has occurred, then the question is: how do we actually knit, or in some way heal, a broken tradition of politics that was based on the hope that our technological and scientific knowledge can actually make the world better – and not just for the wealthy few?

JVC: If one accepts that this tradition is completely broken, then there are pieces of rubble – as you suggested earlier, discussing questions of methodology – that we can pull out, look at again, and think again across this supposed unbridgeable gap. So, what interests me, as well as the juxtapositions of montage, is that this is also addressing the question: to what extent does one accept the fact that the Right can announce the end of History? Or, for instance, that, with the decline of the Soviet Union, the kinds of utopian aspirations that you speak of having seen still active there in 1991 actually can't be sustained, or at least it's very hard for them to be sustained, when the dominant thinking is that this is now relegated to the past. So that's the kind of utopian thinking [which would face the past], an engagement with a tradition of Socialism and the Left, "the radical aspiration," as Annette Michelson has called it.

SBM: Yes, but, of course, precisely because the Soviet experiment is in ruins, we can think of returning to reappropriate aspects of it. Otherwise, we would be bound by its use of state terror to continue to protest against it. The defusing of the dangers posed by the Soviet Union was signaled by the artists of the pre-*glasnost* period, who began to recycle the Soviet symbols as irony and parody – but also, it must be said, as nostalgia, for a dreamworld of socialism that was *supposed* to be.

JVC: Whereas, I suppose, you could argue that the artworks of Komar and Melamid and the other Satirists of the Soviet Union are, in their satire, making an engagement which is both a montage and *also* has something to do with a restitution that you would think is appropriate?

SBM: What I want to insist upon with this notion of montage is that if the Left returns to the past, it is not to redeem some sort of original ideal world from which we have been banished. Not at all. So the nostalgia is really for *the possibility of something else today*, not for what in fact existed in the past. The shattering of time is key, describing "history" – the dreamworld of historical "progress" – as shattered, and consequently a destruction of the conception of time-as-progress on both sides, East and West. The Right calls this the "end of history" and celebrates it. But what about the Left, which looks to the pieces of a shattered past? How can we reassemble them in ways that free us from the triumphalism of the present?

JVC: What's so gripping about this section [II] of *Dreamworld and Catastrophe* is that it discusses historical method, the juxtaposition of these past practices, the juxtaposition of these past fragments with our present concerns which, as you say, might have the power to challenge the complacency of our times. As a political task I thought this was so striking.

SBM: Striking, maybe, but at the moment I'm not terribly optimistic. There is a political question here, and it is part of the pathos of our present historical moment. Benjamin was working on a project about the nineteenth century, while the world was being destroyed around him. There was not time for his "big book" about the Paris arcades; a decade of working on it didn't help to defuse the political emergency of Nazism and World War II. The same holds true today. From a Leftist perspective, going through the rubble of past history is a dubious enterprise given the urgency of the present global situation. I would be hard-pressed to justify it as an effective political weapon at this moment.

JVC: Surely challenging our present's complacency by any political means available to us is a necessity. One way does seem to be through this sense of looking for the materialities of history as a way of seeing into the future. That people can't read your most recent book without saying you're a Stalinist, that people can't think about September 11 without seeing it as a "things will never be the same" afterwards [event] – which is one of the most objectionable pieces of rhetoric, that sense of always trying to make a crisis after which nothing will be the same – when it seems to me that one of the things that the Left has to do now is that instead of building towards the future, it has to build towards the future by trying to rescue the past from these cataclysms.

SBM: I have actually used that objectional phrase, that things will never be the same after September 11, because of the authoritarian US response. I have used that phrase because I wanted to say to Left intellectuals, "stop writing as if only academic politics were at stake! We need to get back to the material, political world."

JVC: Yes I absolutely agree. But I think you're going back to the material world in [. . .] a kind of political, historical, material sense which implies that one shouldn't necessarily accept mythologies in which time is figured in these moments, gaps . . .

SBM: I'm thinking of an image, a photograph of *Trümmerfrauen* in Berlin after World War II – women who set about cleaning up the ruins after the military devastation, dusting off the bricks from shattered buildings, piling them up to be recycled as material for rebuilding. Sometimes I feel I am doing the same . . .

JVC: Two things. One, you're in a Department of Government in a top US university, and that puts you in a much stronger position to be able to respond more directly via whatever media and other forms are available. [. . .] And two, one doesn't have to write about particular topics, politics let's say, to have their impact, the impact of politics, infuse one's writing.

SBM: Let's not be utopian. I'm in a Political Philosophy sub-field of a Government Department, and some of my colleagues wish that I wouldn't write about Soviet Studies, which is not my field, but, rather, teach and write intellectual biographies of the Frankfurt School. That is, I shouldn't *use* critical theory, I should teach it. The fact that I do use it may be a strength of my work, but it is also its academic vulnerability.

JVC: In old-fashioned terms that means you're functioning as an intellectual and not an academic.

SBM: I would like to think so. As far as it is possible. But the way neo-liberalism has affected university culture, at least in the United States, is to discourage one from being an intellectual who contributes to public debate, and to train "professional" academics instead. There's a world of difference between the two. Neo-liberalism's idea of intellectual life is that in the great marketplace of ideas, everyone expresses her or his "opinion," no matter how ignorant it is, while academics are useful only as human data-banks.

JVC: I like the idea of academic vulnerability. It seems to have something to do with leaving yourself open, which can bring on two very different potential responses: the first is that it might instigate dialogue, which is nice, while the second is the inevitable attack and subsequent mauling of the one making themselves vulnerable, defenceless. But the idea is the right one.

SBM: Well, let's look at that possibility [of academic vulnerability being something positive]. Assuming that there is a political advantage in developing a methodology that avoids a certain kind of academic culture, what, then – getting back to the question of the

Left, and of its disappearance, or its impotence – can a method that looks backward do? Can it have an effect on the present situation?

JVC: I would say that this is very much what it has to do. It has to reverse its presumption. That is, it has to reverse the presumption that out of a utopian expectation you look towards the future. To a certain extent now I think your implication is that if the utopian aspiration can no longer be a driving intellectual force, then to a certain extent it's progressive to look backwards. And that gets you away from nostalgia and so on. Although nostalgia itself always has a bad press, it might just mean a more sentimental side of the desire to try and recuperate moments of hope from the past.

Media, the Global Public Sphere, Community

JVC: What impact do you think new communication technologies, from email to hand-held video cameras, are having on our sense of experiencing the contemporary world as a specifically global environment?

SBM: If we take the example of September 11, we can certainly speak of a global media, as opposed to a transnational media. The difference is that the space of global media is immanent, which means that you cannot separate or segregate national publics. In World War II, governments pretty much had control over the means of production of propaganda for their own people, and they generated propaganda specifically to demoralize the other side. Today there is no longer a geographical dividing line between "sides"; these media spaces are integrated, overlapping, and multiple. As a weapon of resistance, the medium of the internet can operate at low altitudes, connecting people under the radar screen of government censors, while satellite TV flies in above the censors. The very existence of al-Jazeera, the Arab version of CNN, has had a tremendous impact in shaping what we can call a global public sphere. Not only are 35 million people in the Middle East watching it, but increasing numbers of people through satellite connections *inside* the United States (and elsewhere) as well. Even if the language is Arabic, the images are accessible to a global public, and the US government can't do anything to destroy its impact. This is new since the [first] Gulf War, when the US monopolized global representations of international politics far more successfully. I don't know of any political occasion prior to the present when we've experienced such a superimposition of media spaces, such a lack of controlling center.

JVC: About access to information in the USA, on the one hand there's a shutdown on the part of the government which prevents information from flowing freely, and there seems to be quite a lot of support for the government's rhetoric – the "either you're with us or against us" position – but on the other hand there are people watching al-Jazeera because they want the information. Of course these may well just be different groupings of people!

SBM: Or the same people, increasingly schizophrenic! If you get your news from alternative sources on the net, you would think you were in a different world from the one presented to the US by commercial media. I receive mails from Egyptian feminist organizations and from RAWA, the revolutionary feminists of Afghanistan, with information that cuts through the PR nonsense of the Bush administration posing as the liberator of Muslim women. We don't know how widely these messages are being disseminated. It takes a local demonstration to bring all the net-radicals out of the closet, but when that happens it gives a glimmer of the enormous potential. There is considerable Left-organizing power via the web that is only now being tested. The Chiapas revolt used internet communication successfully to create global solidarity. With September 11, the stakes are higher, while communication is more difficult, given the appalling ignorance in the US regarding Islamism and the Arab world. And the dangers are greater, given the extreme potential for violence. Of course, internet publics can be monitored, but with millions involved, how realistic is that? There is so much information on the web, and no one to read it all. I find the excess comforting. It's a political safety feature.

JVC: Do you believe that we can think about this whole area of exchange, of letter writing, messaging, as a modern public sphere? Is it a new form of the public sphere? What, also, about this question of the global public intellectual? Is it possible for something like this to exist? And what does it mean for you as an intellectual, as someone who tries to be a practicing public intellectual, and works on globalization, to be involved in a global public sphere?

SBM: We need to work with this concept – a global public sphere – as a place for politics. Since September 11, it seems vital to question the "think global, act local" slogan of Left politics in the 1990s. We have to act globally as well. But this is an extremely difficult matter, as there is no agreement regarding the discursive terrain. There is no already-existing global space that one might enter in order to engage in violence-free communication, to use Habermas' phrase. We need to build that space, and one way is, performatively, to address it. What does the "Left" look like in a global public sphere? Can we even use this term?

To speak of the global is to speak about media. And, of course, a mediated community is not a community in the traditional sense of living together, working together. The collective spirit produced by media is fairly superficial. Empathic identifications are instantaneous, but they can just as instantaneously disappear. Without language in common, the global public sphere will have to rely heavily on images. It will be a visual culture – or musical, perhaps, but not dominantly print.

If we are talking about a global Left today, the 1960s is surely the precursor. The music, for example – John Lennon's song "Imagine" was censored from the airwaves in the US after September 11 [the same song has been movingly present during mass demonstrations in Israel against Sharon's brutal policies toward Palestinians]. The V for victory sign was appropriated as a peace sign in the 60s; the raised fist signified growing radicalization. You saw these visual markers in demonstrations – in photographs of demonstrations – in Mexico City, Athens, Tokyo, Berkeley, Berlin. And you had the sense that with the mimetic spread of even this very small gesture, global solidarity was being built around a set of issues: anti-imperialism, anti-racism, pro-national liberation. It might be argued that if the demonstrators had actually been in the same room together, they might not have understood each other's concrete concerns – although I'm not so sure. The imagined community of the 1960s was indeed a global social movement. Political solidarity transcended national boundaries. When the African-American medal winners at the 1968 Olympics in Mexico City raised their fists on the winners' podium, this image, in this context, was montaged with images of demonstrating students shot by government troops on the streets of Mexico City the week before – that was a very powerful media intervention. I am not aware of research in visual culture that has dealt with this prehistory of today's global public sphere. Such a study would be valuable. Again, this is history-writing with a political function.

Such a history would show that global and local politics are not necessarily in contradiction. Today's media magnify the potential for synergy. Ithaca, where Cornell is located, is a Left-political, small town, where community newspapers, distributed for free, combine articles downloaded from the web with political commentary by local writers – and reprints from the past (Marx's "11 Theses on Feuerbach" appeared, with the suggestion that readers clip it for their refrigerator doors!). After September 11, faculty and students organized a Cornell Forum for Justice and Peace with a website and listserve. We are a documentation and information collective that serves as an interface connecting global and local action. This kind of politics is being established all over the world, producing a counter-culture that might support a global Left with strong roots in local communities. We don't know at the moment how successful such a movement might be, whether it can resist the global hegemony that has such a dominant position within commercial media. This is the first great political test of the new media, and I am optimistic . . . but cautiously.

BIBLIOGRAPHY

Ahmad, Aijaz. *In the Mirror of Urdu: Recompositions of Nation and Community 1947–1965*. Rashtrapati Nivas, Shimla, 1993.

Ahmed, Akbar S. *Postmodernism and Islam: Predicament and Promise*. New York and London: Routledge, 1996.

Ahmed, Leila. *Women and Gender in Islam: Historical Roots of a Modern Debate*. New Haven: Yale University Press, 1992.

Arkoun, Mohammed. *Rethinking Islam: Common Questions, Uncommon Answers*. Trans. and ed. Robert D. Lee. Oxford: Westview Press, 1994.

Asad, Talal, ed. *Anthropology and the Colonial Encounter* [1978]. Amherst, N.Y.: Humanity Books, 1998.

Asad, Talal. *Genealogies of Religion: Discipline and Reasons of Power in Christianity and Islam*. Baltimore and London: The Johns Hopkins University Press, 1993.

Ataman, Kutlug. "Semiha B Unplugged," video film, 1997.

Benjamin, Walter. *Illuminations.* Ed. Hannah Arendt, trans. Harry Zohn. New York: Schocken Books, 1968.

Brennan, Teresa. *Exhausting Modernity: Grounds for a New Economy.* New York and London: Routledge, 2000.

—— *Globalization and its Terrors.* New York and London: Routledge, 2002.

—— *Transmission of Affect.* Ithaca: Cornell University Press, 2003.

Buck-Morss, Susan. *The Dialectics of Seeing: Walter Benjamin and the Arcades Project.* Cambridge, Mass. and London: The MIT Press, 1989.

—— *Dreamworld and Catastrophe: The Passing of Mass Utopia in East and West.* Cambridge, Mass. and London: The MIT Press, 2000.

—— "Hegel and Haiti." *Critical Inquiry,* 26,4 (Summer 2000): 821–65.

Chomsky, Noam. *9–11,* New York: Seven Stories Press, 2001.

Cooke, Miriam. *Women Claim Islam: Creating Islamic Feminism through Literature.* New York and London: Routledge, 2001.

Davutoglu, Ahmet. "Philosophical and Institutional Dimensions of Secularisation: A Comparative Analysis." In John L. Esposito and Azzam Tamimi, eds. *Islam and Secularism in the Middle East.* New York: New York University Press, 2000. Pp. 170–208.

Eisenstein, Zillah. "Feminisms in the Aftermath of September 11." *Social Text 72,* 20,3 (Fall 2002): 79–100.

—— *Who is the West? Feminisms, Slaveries, Democracies, Islamisms.* London: Zed Books, 2004.

Esposito, John L., ed. *Political Islam: Revolution, Radicalism, or Reform?* London: Lynne Rienner Publishers, 1997.

Esposito, John L. and John O. Voll. *Islam and Democracy.* New York and Oxford: Oxford University Press, 1996.

Euben, Roxanne. L. *Enemy in the Mirror: Islamic Fundamentalism and the Limits of Modern Rationalism.* Princeton: Princeton University Press, 2001.

Foucault, Michel. *The History of Sexuality*, vol. 1: *An Introduction.* Trans. Robert Hurley. New York: Vintage/Ramdom House, 1980.

Al-Ghannouchi, Rachid. "Secularism in the Arab Maghreb." In Azzam Tamimi and John L. Esposito, eds. *Islam and Secularism in the Middle East.* New York: New York University Press, 2000. Pp. 97–123.

Göle, Nilüfer. *The Forbidden Modern: Civilization and Veiling.* Ann Arbor: University of Michigan Press, 1996.

Hardt, Michael and Antonio Negri. *Empire.* Cambridge, Mass. and London: Harvard University Press, 2000.

Hirschkind, Charles and Saba Mahmood, "Feminism, the Taliban, and Politics of Counter-Insurgency." *Anthropological Quarterly* 75, 2 (Spring 2002): 339–54.

Hofstadter, Richard. *The Paranoid Style in American Politics and Other Essays.* New York: Alfred A. Knopf, 1965.

Hudson, Michael C., ed. *Middle East Dilemma: The Politics and Economics of Arab Integration.* New York: Columbia University, 1999.

Huntington, Samuel P. *The Clash of Civilizations and the Remaking of World Order.* New York: Simon and Schuster, 1996.

Iqbal, Muhammad. *The Reconstruction of Religious Thought in Islam* [1944]. Chicago: Kazi Publications; Reprint edition, 1999.

Khan, Muhammad Akram. "Islamic Economics: The State of the Art." *The American Journal of Islamic Social Sciences* 16, 2: 89–104.

Kaya, Ibrahim. "Modernity and Veiled Women." *European Journal of Social Theory* 3 (2): 195–214.

[Al-Khomeini, Imam Ruhullah al-Musavi.] *Islam and Revolution:*

Writings and Declarations of Imam Khomeini. Trans. Hamid Algar. Berkeley: Mizan Press, 1981.

Mahmood, Saba. "Feminist Theory, Embodiment, and the Docile Agent: Some Reflections on the Egyptian Islamic Revival." *Cultural Anthropology* 16(2): 202–36.

Meriwether, Margaret L and Judith E. Tucker, eds. *Social History of Women and Gender in the Modern Middle East.* Boulder: Westview Press, 1999.

El-Messiri, Abdelwahab. "Secularism, Immanence and Deconstruction." In John L. Esposito and Azzam Tamimi, eds. *Islam and Secularism in the Middle East.* New York: New York University Press, 2000. Pp. 52–80.

Mignolo, Walter D. *The Darker Side of the Renaissance: Literacy, Territoriality, and Colonization.* Ann Arbor: The University of Michigan Press, 2000.

Mir-Hosseini, Ziba. *Islam and Gender: The Religious Debate in Contemporary Iran.* Princeton: Princeton University Press, 1999.

Mirsepassi, Ali. *Intellectual Discourse and the Politics of Modernization: Negotiating Modernity in Iran.* New York and Cambridge: Cambridge University Press, 2000.

Mohanty, Chandra Talpade, Ann Russo, and Lourdes Torres, eds. *Third World Women and the Politics of Feminism.* Bloomington: Indiana University Press, 1991.

Mousalli, Ahmed S. "Discourses on Human Rights and Pluralistic Democracy." In *Islam in a Changing World.* Pp. 45–89.

Osborne, Peter. *Philosophy in Cultural Theory.* New York and London: Routledge, 2000.

Qutb, Sayyid. *Social Justice in Islam.* Oneanta: Islamic Publications International, 2000.

Rahman, Fazlur. *Islam and Modernity: Transformation of an Intellectual Tradition.* Chicago: The University of Chicago Press, 1982.

Roy, Olivier, *The Failure of Political Islam*. Trans. Carol Volk. Cambridge, Mass. and London: Harvard University Press, 1994.

Said, Edward. *Orientalism*. New York: Pantheon, 1978.

—— *Peace and its Discontents: Essays on Palestine in the Middle East Peace Process*. Preface Christopher Hitchens. New York: Vintage Books, 1996.

Salamé, Ghassan, ed. *Democracy without Democrats? The Renewal of Politics in the Muslim World*. New York and London: I.B. Tauris 2001.

Sánchez, Oswaldo, and Cecilia Garza, eds. *Fugitive Sites: inSITE2000/ 01. New Contemporary Art Projects for San Diego/Tijuana*. San Diego: Installation Gallery, 2003.

Sayyid, Bobby S. *A Fundamental Fear: Eurocentrism and the Emergence of Islamism*. London: Zed Books, 1997.

Sharabi, Hisham. *Arab Intellectuals and the West: The Formative Years, 1875–1914*. Baltimore: The Johns Hopkins University Press, 1970.

—— *Neopatriarchy: A Theory of Distorted Change in Arab Society*. New York and Oxford: Oxford University Press, 1988.

—— ed. *Theory, Politics, and the Arab World*. New York and London: Routledge, 1990.

[Shariati, Ali] *Shariati on Shariati and the Muslim Woman*. Ed. Laleh Bakhtiar. Chicago: Kazi/ABC International, 1996.

Taha, Mahmoud Mohamed. *The Second Message of Islam*. Syracuse: Syracuse University Press, 1996.

Tamáss: Comtemporary Arab Representations. Intro. Catherine David. Barcelona: Fundació Antoni Tàpies, 2002.

Tamimi, Azzam S. *Rachid Ghannouchi: A Democrat within Islam*. New York and Oxford: Oxford University Press, 2001.

Tibi, Bassam. *The Challenge of Fundamentalism: Political Islam and* the *New World Disorder*. Berkeley: University of California Press, 1998.

Turner, Bryan S. *Marx and the End of Orientalism*. London: George Allen and Unwin, 1978.

Zulaika, Joseba and William A. Douglass. *Terror and Taboo: The Follies, Fables, and Faces of Terrorism*. New York and London: Routledge, 1996.

INDEX